LAW OF FIRST THOUGHT

A Guide to Understanding the Power of Your Mind

Rosewitha G. Shelton

RGS Publications

Copyright 2017

LAW OF FIRST THOUGHT

A Guide to Understanding the Power of Your Mind

RGS Publications

LAW OF FIRST THOUGHT
A Guide to Understanding the Power of Your Mind

Copyright © 2017 RGS Publications

All rights reserved. No part of this book may be reproduced by any means, graphic, electronic, or mechanical, including photocopying, recording, taping or by any information storage retrieval system without the written permission of the publisher except in the case of brief quotations embodied in critical articles and reviews.

RGS Publications books may be ordered through booksellers or by contacting:

RGS Publishing
P.O. Box 92860
Washington, DC 20090

ISBN: 978-0-9857188-7-9

RGS Publications

Printed in the United States of America

First Printing: May 20, 2017

Dedication

I dedicate this book, as all of my productions, to my husband and children, both tangible and intangible. I thank you because you love me just the way I am. I thank you because who you are makes me be the greatest possibility of myself. I thank you because I experience the greatest love and possibilities of God through you. I thank you for being the beauty, perfection and joy of life every time you breathe. I love you more than words are able to express.

Table of Contents

Dedication	i
PART I – THOUGHT	**1**
A Thought Was Born	2
I Think I Must Protect Who I Don't Remember I Am	6
I Am What I Know	11
Know	16
Experience There	18
Can You Feel It	23
PART II – LAW	**27**
In the Beginning	28
Become Aware	30
I Am Like God	31
I Am the Truth and the Light	33
What Is Law	34
Original Thought	37
Lord's Prayer	38
Meditate on These Things	39
Sow and Receive	42
Seed	43
Speak a Thing	45
PART III -- SPEAK CO-CREATOR	**47**
Honesty Can Set You Free	48
My Power to Speak Works for Me	50

Whatever You Say Shall Be	52
Your Power Is Where You Say It Is	54
PART IV - FEAR	**57**
Fear Is Feedback	58
Fear in the Shadows	60
Self-Deception of the Second Nature	63
Everlasting Fear	66
Fear of Change	69
PART V - EXPERIENCE IS A LIAR AND YET HOLDS ALL TRUTH	**73**
Experience Speaks	74
I Create from Experience	81
Experience Is Not Always a Great Teacher	83
PART VI – THE WORK	**85**
Question the Thought	86
Forgive	87
Do You First Love Yourself	88
I Am Whole	91
Your Prayer Is Your Wish,	92
So Wish Wisely	92
PART VII– RESPONSIBILITY	**95**
Choose Ye This Day	96
Judge Not, But In All Things,	96
Be Wise As A Serpent	96
God Is No Respecter of Person or Thought	98

PART I – THOUGHT

A Thought Was Born

> When I was a child I thought like a child and when I became a man, I put away childish ways.
>
> —1 Corinthians 13:11

Your specific personality and belief system within your mind was conditioned and nurtured by the lineage, culture, community, country, religion, and home environment in which you grew up.

Who you are and will be was etched in stone from the age of zero to eight years old and was then built upon from thereafter. Over time, thoughts and experiences affected the belief system creating some variances to who you are and will become; but overall, your belief system remains true to what formed it in the beginning stages of your life until it can believe in something even greater than the past idea it found to be real or true.

What is even more amazing is that this eight-year-old foundation of your physical self's consciousness drives most of your life, even though it actually holds questionable concepts of reality from a child's perspective molded by others still trying to figure out their own journey of self. The truths it finds itself believing in, is actually instead, a reflection of a small space of time the physical self-experienced and found to be true because the experiences felt more real than what it knew in Spirit before it was born.

Before braving this physical possibility of yourself, you were initially only a Spirit. A spirit untouched or phased with the limitation of the physical. A being of energy indifferent to the happenings and conditions of outside thoughts or experiences. You were perfect in all aspects of the possibilities of you. In this form, you were the holder of truth and limitless godness. You were a creator decided, with a thought to manifest itself into human form. Not to test yourself or punish yourself, but

Law of First Thought

because you knew that no matter what form you became, it did not take away from the greatness of who you are. It would, in fact, further prove this truth of being absolute.

Sometimes you have to know or experience the contradiction of something to accept it without doubt. The contradiction often helps you to better understand and solidify what is thought or perceived to be true. The contradiction can often become the evidence. Sometimes you cannot know something for sure without experience. Knowledge is not always enough; however, through experience knowledge becomes wisdom.

Understanding this, you touched the God within you, created a vision of you and then spoke the word to experience the concept of a human being with the power of your godness available to you. Have you ever thought about the marriage of the human physical matter and the Spirit being both existing as one in you?

When you started this path of transition to man, Spirit agreed with your idea of you and in co-creation, your path was made. Transformation into matter began. You thought your vision of self into being with the power of an even greater force of thought; this force of thought we often call God, the Universe, Spirit or some other infinite equality; and you were made so. The contract and vision that co-creation created manifested as you.

This is how powerful you are. Powerful enough to be born of a thought. A thought of possibility accepted and agreed upon in co-creation with you and your Creator. You were powerful enough to realize that any path of life given or taken cannot change the power you are and no experience can overcome the true source of greatness you know to be true. And yet, today, you do not remember who you are. Today, you have forgotten. Today, the physical has overcome the spirit. Today, you seek what you already have, because you think it or you are lost. You look for what you already know because you've learned not to trust or believe in you. You struggle with what you have already overcome; because you bought into the weakness of the flesh journey you call life. You fear the unknown and dread the known.

Despite this truth about you, you feel powerless in your day- to - day situations, circumstances and relationships. You can, because you are that contradiction right now. You know that you are able to rise out of any ashes you birth your way into and somehow you are not sure how it is possible when you exam your earthly capability. Your vision has been focused on the wrong aspect of you. You have forgotten to use the power within you to rise up out of ashes. The ashes of life and circumstances you once saw as just something to pass through on your way to your greatest desire. How could you know without a shadow of a doubt who you were in the face and seat of God, be birthed by a human and forsake your likeness of God for the likeness of a human? Man, a body suit lost on his way, convinces you that being lost is normal and being like God is blasphemous. Now, you sit in the midst of a desert trying to figure out if you are worthy enough to walk into the promised land you created, imagined, asked and have been given because man spoke and did things to foster a childlike limited existence of you. You allowed men to speak and define you after your creator has already spoken. After the amazing co-creation between you and your Creator you sit in the desert weighing man's words and deeds as if they hold validity more so than the one who created you.

We struggle with this thought – Who Am I? Which narrative should I accept of myself and which to deny? We struggle and struggle and yet we do not know why we struggle. We are afraid to act and afraid to think the thoughts that will stop the struggle. We have become the struggle of our minds. We live the confusion of our minds. Our life is a reflection of the struggle, which is why we cannot conjure an answer to "Who Am I?" We have become the likeness and image of the confusion. We are bound by our own mind and the fear of constant unanswered questions. We are confused by the face of normality, of the struggle and constant questioning within and all around us.

We should be able to find the answer within. However, we have not mastered a relationship with ourselves to know ourselves, so we search for the answers outside of us. Only to discover that those outside of us that we often perceive to know more than we do, they too still struggle themselves as to who they are.

This struggle is found at the foundation of our society. Many people in our society are often doing anything it takes in order to receive validation, attention and notoriety to make themselves feel good or important. The drive to know who we are through the eyes, mouths and attention of others is a misguided and distorted concept that directs to the root of our real issues. If we need others to tell us who we are, it is because we do not know. The problem with others telling us, is that they are usually only reflecting back to us-- who we think we are. So if we think we are nothing, they treat us, tell us and look at us in that same manner – like nothing. We teach people not only how to treat us, but how to look at us, talk to us and speak to us.

To return things back into balance, you have to come into the realization and self-actualization of who you are. We do this by becoming brave enough to ask the right questions of ourselves and receive the true answers. The questions that not only help us to understand who we are, but also how we got here to this point. We got here because of what we thought. Our lives are the way they are, because of what we still think. We have thought our way into being. For example, we do not work our way out of poverty, we think our way out of poverty and into success. We think our way into healthy relationships and out of dysfunctional relationships. We think and therefore we become. We thought and therefore became. Who are you? You are a thought, imagined by you and supported with the laws of creation gifted by your creator. You become what you imagined. You did not become what you thought was impossible for you or someone like you. That is because your mind and your creator love you enough to give you only what you believe and think you can handle. Not what you hope or wish, but what is in reflection and relationship to your belief of you. Your thought is the driving force of your will and possibility.

Part I - Thought

I Think I Must Protect Who I Don't Remember I Am

Because you are thought, all that you do or don't do is based on thoughts you have and thoughts created from experiences you have had, seen or heard. Experiences that have impacted you through one of your five senses. As a child, your experiences as a human become the most real and mind blowing to your Spirit. We must remember there are two aspects of ourselves, human self and spirit self. Your Spirit is still connected to the unlimited possibilities of the universe. However, through your five senses it experiences itself with limitations as a human. In this duality of yourself, the Spirits unlimited and powerful beingness can often be overshadow by the realities of life's earthly limits because the tangible feels more real than the unseen. The tangible definitions of life experiences begin to move to the forefront of your mind, and become the storyteller of whom you are and who you are not.

In this place of duality, thoughts of greatness, importance and possibility become challenged. Not only challenged, but also crushed. Not only by your thoughts, but also by the very people you thought would be your protectors, guides, and assistors on earth for and with you.

Contradictions, disappointment and confusion cause you to question everything to the point, in your infinite power with infancy wisdom; you create a belief system geared toward protection more than manifestation and actualization. The thought that I need to protect myself; creates just that. A life of protecting one's life, heart, soul, path, decisions, etc. Protection becomes the driving force and resulting limiting enclosure, leading and guiding choice and belief. When you manifest out of protection, you have created from a spirit of fear that holds the distortions of life's experiences and not the depth of the spiritual realities of yourself.

This is a reason we begin to not trust ourselves as much as those and that around you. We want others to tell us to trust our steps, that the coast is clear, and we are ready enough to move ahead because we are too busy worrying about failing, hurt, pain and feeling life. We are fearful and need someone else to help us and to blame for how we feel, the choices we make and the falls we take. If we have to do it alone and trust ourselves, we would have to be responsible and that's scary. It puts too many things into question and humans don't like questions. We are taught from children to stop asking so many questions. We get nervous when we are questioned, especially if we are not sure of the answer. We also fear the changes that may come when the answer to the question is realized. This is a natural fear fostered for generations starting from childhood.

One of the things that are hardest for many of us to accept is that the mind and its process we struggle to change in our adult life is actually that of an eight- or nine-year-old. This child consciousness stands guard of our mind's overall processing system. To change the system, you have to deal with this child who stands guard of the system it helped create and has maintained all of its life. The mind has limits that it will not allow you to override, overcome, stretch, or break through. However, if you can prove that you believe without doubt that change in thought is for the ultimate benefit and good of you, it will allow change.

Remember you are thought held by thought. As long as you believe you need protection, the protector created by you will not cease from existing. It will do the job it was created to do. You now have to change the thought that you no longer need protection, or change the manner of operation of the protector that your belief system believes it cannot literally live without. Remember nothing ever really dies, it only changes form or direction. This is true of the guard once he is created.

The guard believes it is doing its job of protection by believing in the thoughts of old. It will work on the walls of its existence and thoughts when it senses belief systems are beginning to crack, weaken, or contort. It has mastered this act of shoring up old beliefs over the years, longer than your awareness of its ability.

In order to create change, the mind must create a thought the gatekeeper, the child, can accept as more real and acceptable than the thought on which the gatekeeper has survived. The new walls of thought must prove to be better and more reliable than the old. The old walls of thought must be torn down and new walls have to be built. You cannot have two opposing walls of thought; you can only have one or the other. However, you cannot tear down one wall without replacing it with another - lest the building fall and create a mental, emotional or spiritual breakdown. The breakdown in the mind leads to a breakdown in the body. The protector knows this and that is why the mind holds fast to itself as is. That is why the gatekeeper stays busy to maintain homeostasis; it loves to protect you that much. It has good intentions; it will not allow you to fall, even if it has to use old thoughts to maintain you.

Never despise the protector of you. Appreciate it, understand it - so you can utilize it for your good. Awareness of the gatekeeper and its role can help you become empowered. Realize you are not in a battle with yourself, the gatekeeper or anything outside of you. This is self-evident that you are powerful enough to create on your behalf. In this awareness, realize further that what you create, you can destroy, change and recreate. Stop wrestling with YOU, embrace yourself, love yourself into a new place, and love your protector into its new role of assisting you in the building of your new belief system and resulting new life.

Thought is the only tool your protector uses and the only tool you have to make changes in your life. Thoughts create other thoughts. If we allow fear to associate with those thoughts, then fear will lead and guide every aspect of our lives. In order to get a different experience and change the compass of our direction, we must create and feed the protector new thoughts that also change the job description of the protector to assistant of the new creation of you and your life.

Law of First Thought

Until you get the protector on your side as assistant to make the necessary changes in your belief system, then no change will occur. Every move forward will end up taking you right back to the place of homeostasis. You cannot just think a new thought, you must believe that new thought so much that it is strong enough to uphold and take over from the old one and be accepted by the protector of your mind's system. If you do not first believe in the thought, the protector of the belief system will not either. It will not allow you to replace a thought it cannot trust to hold you and keep you safe on your journey. Remember that the protector has only been empowered through the thoughts and experiences of childhood and the life thereafter. It does not remember the truth of who you were prior to the journey because you have forsaken feeding the thoughts of who you were prior to the protector's creation. As you forget, so does the protector. As you remember, so the protector is reconnected to the power that you are and it conforms to the truth of that knowledge.

At times, you may think you are being failed by your mind when you can't let go of old habits and relationships. But your mind thinks it is helping you by staying in the confinement of its protection—that which it is comfortable and used to. Consciously, you know it is horrible, but the mind's system thinks it is upholding your first nature. It is the only nature in relationship it knows, the physical you. It is maintaining the status quo of yesterday. Since it knows how to help you heal and get over certain things, it does not want to create another situation it won't know how to deal with. Until you are confident change is necessary and beneficial, nothing changes. Even if it appears to change in the moment, nothing really changes until the belief system itself changes. It cannot change. It is against the law of creation and existence to change without the belief of greater benefit and assured ability to cope with the change. It will not fail you by changing without these assurances. It will remain the same for what is perceived to be the reliable with which you are comfortable, despite there being no actual reliability at all.

Part I - Thought

Comfort and knowing are perceptions of good, not because they are by nature good, but because by nature you know it. You find it trustworthy; therefore, you give it the nature of good. All that you know in relationship and experience is in direct correlation with your vision and beliefs and therefore in line with the nature given to it by the creator or co-creator, which is you. All that you create is perceived good. All that you allow your attention to hold and believe in is perceived as beneficially good by law because by law you are good and beneficial by nature. Because you see yourself in this noble position, all that you create is in your likeness is good and worthy for you. You cannot create anything contrary to your own nature.

Until you can provide the system with a better and more improved option in which to believe, it won't change. The mind's system will work against the change. This is not a bad thing. It is just the law in operation. It is how the mind is programmed to work on your behalf. It is a testament to the mind's and the thoughts of the mind's power and ability. The mind is just doing its job. So you have to do yours to get the mind to change for your benefit. Otherwise, the mind will keep resetting and rebooting its processing belief system to its original state, until you establish and trust that the old system and its employed thoughts are no longer a benefit to hold on to. You must believe that greater is meant and intended for you and you are worthy and believe in the truth of who you are and were before you were placed in your mother's womb and birthed through the experiences you have had. Then and only then will the old thoughts and resulting mind's belief system, make room for the new thoughts and create a new belief system that will manifest a new life.

I Am What I Know

You cannot know what you have never had. And you cannot have what you have never known. You only know what you have had. Therefore, you continue to recreate what is familiar to you. Here is the thing, in all universal reality there is nothing you have never had or cannot have. The universe is one with you and when you ask, all is given to you. But what is given, is not being created when you ask. It is already created and has already been given for you to have. Nothing is denied you, all is yours. It has only been waiting on you to become aware of it, receive it and then ask and allow it to manifest. When you ask for it to move from your awareness to manifestation, the process begins. You are not waiting for anything, it is actually waiting for you to see, recognize, accept, believe and then ask for what already is.

So though you have not known a thing in physical existence, you have known all things, which is why you can have all things. However, your failure in awareness of that which is beyond your experience makes it an unknown. As an unknown, it is not in your ability to see. If you cannot see it as a possibility, then it cannot be touched in your imagination for you to accept, ask and then receive. So you keep seeing and therefore receiving what you have already known. The experiences are common, normal, known and expected.

Until you create and then form a new vision of and for yourself through the possibilities of your thoughts, feelings, and mind, the old thoughts remain as the directors of your creative possibility. You are the creator, the master potter on the wheel of your life. You can change the clay formation whenever and however you desire, or keep it as it is. That is a gift of choice given to you by the creator.

One of the things that I did not get for a long time is why my life and so many others' lives stopped progressing or stagnated at certain points no matter how much they worked, gave or tried. There was a plateau. Many times, for generations, you are able to see a pattern unbroken by time, deeds, distance or awareness. No matter how much success or how much it appeared the cycles of lineage broken, somehow, someway, when things settled, one person after another would reach or fall to a level of existence that no one in the family or around them appear to be able to excel beyond. So I asked Spirit to help me understand this. This is what Spirit revealed to me. It said that *I and the Father Are One. We, human spirit and the Spirit of God, are in constant co-creation. We all are. The problem is that most of us do not believe it so we forsake using the power that is ours. Often humans are waiting for the power to operate on their behalf without their participation and operation in the law. Instead of intentional creation, we humans are creating without intent. We are creating with hope and hope is not the same thing as intentional belief and often holds in sight what it wants to get away from, but not what it truly desires. However, what you see and pay attention to is what is receiving the power of creation to manifest. Therefore, you continue to recreate what you actually do not desire. Spirit said that the mind is like a bowl in which the hand of the human spirit, and the creator's hand come together to create and manifest that which is desired. This can be a thing, a state of being, etc.*

Spirit says that Spirit has already given an unlimited possibility of existence for the human spirit, but in the mind, Spirit has also given the human spirit free will to create and free choice to choose what it shall think and believe. Therefore, humanity is leading in creation for themselves. They are using the power of God given to them to do so, but the human spirit is given authority over itself. What is happening in process is that the human spirit is failing to see the unlimited possibilities through Spirit; instead, humans choose to focus on their human limitations and fail to see or remember the spirit part of themselves that is not limited or defined by the humanity of their experience. This distortion of the true vision of self is what is limiting and determining the manifestation of human life. It is all about what we believe.

Law of First Thought

The human's constrained image and uncertainty of self is born out of a failing confidence fostered by what has been humanly experienced, expressed and cultivated by and through the hands of not only the human itself, but also by other humans plagued by the same contaminations of thought. A lowly focus mastered through the lineage of existence that can only reconstruct after its own likeness. Which is why it keeps repeating itself. Hu-Man does not know whom he really is which is why he does not know what to believe in.

To change the foresight and stretch it beyond what has already been done, the human spirit has to see what God sees and allow that image of unlimited possibility lead. Even if the visual revelation does not make sense and does not match what is factually known by man now. It only has to make sense and be received through Spirit alone to be placed in the process for manifestation. Because God has gifted us choice and will not override our choice, we have to be responsible in making sound choices in what we think, see and believe. Because we have the ability to contaminate the bowl of creation. Having human experiences distort the truth of life, promises and what we can do and have.

With this in mind, we realize that we, the human spirit, place our hand in the bowl of creation often contaminated with doubt, wonder, confusion, limitations, fears, lies and man-made obstacles. This contamination gets in the midst of the intentional creation and impacts the matter of manifestation. Our human spirit hand is in the bowl with the clear and unlimited possibilities of God's hand, and instead of conceding to that greatness, he sees, believes and brings to us to see and agree upon, we allow the otherness on our hands to muddy the water.

In co-creation where we have been given power, authority and our own will we lead the conversation and God's power in us is utilized to operate on our behalf in accordance to the richest and glory we see and believe. So limited sight and belief only allows us to receive and tap into limited places of God and therefore limits us.

Spirit says that when we humans speak, God speaks; what and when we believe, God believes with us, and what we see, God sees as well. Moreover, in co-creation God says "yes" to what I speak, believe and see. The universe does not override your power of creation; it works with it and agrees with our belief. There is no fight with God, it is only with ourselves and what we consider true.

Yes, we are that powerful and have that much responsibility. Only we can stop the contaminated thoughts and experiences. Only we can change the vision. Only we can change our words. Only we can change our thoughts to mirror the unlimited truth of the creator so that what we co-create is beyond any limitation life has created and beyond the thoughts resulting from those experiences and outside systems of belief.

We choose what to believe in. There is always a thought, a belief system in place that is directing our life. If the old one is not overthrown by a new and stronger one, then the old one remains in power creating on our behalf in the place of power over our choice and creation.

But how do we create what we have never had and do not know despite it being available to us? Let's use peace as an example. When you have never experienced peace, you have to create peace in your mind's imagination. In God, all things are possible, so you have to go to the place of co-creation with God, create what has seemed impossible to this point, and imagine it as the real and only possibility before you. You have to imagine and create what you think peace looks, feels and sounds like. In the secret place of creation, the mind does not judge in value, but it also does not judge whether the thing is physically real or imagined, because all things created in the heaven of your mind is real right now in Spirit, and therefore truth. The mind's secret place just takes it as your creation in heaven that shall be formed in order to manifest. Everything in the mind is real to the universe. Everything you think upon is possible. If you don't believe me, try it. Where the mind goes, the body goes and so does your life.

Imagine peace, and see how your body feels as you lay in the imagination of your mind's peace. Then imagine someone murdering you, feel the heaviness, the struggle as if it were happening to you. Feel the pain and helplessness. Hear the sounds of murder and the anger and uncertainty. Taste the staleness of the room and the closing in of darkness around you. Realize that as you imagine this in your mind as a real occurrence happening to you at this moment, not like a movie being watched, but a real occurrence happening to you and your body right now. Notice how the imaged feeling takes over your body. Your imagination is powerful enough to create energy responses that make a thing real to you. If you were to continue to recreate this image and draw yourself into situations in which this was possible, you could think and believe yourself into a situation. Not guaranteeing your murder, but definitely walking on the line enough to draw something negative to you. The universe does not decide which we will think or choose to think upon, we do that. If you choose peace and partake in walks in your imagination in this state, you create it to be manifested in your regular experience. You are saying to the universe; this is who I am. This is how I see myself. This state is what brings me greater joy. This state I give my attention and energy to. The universe agrees with you like a genie, your wish is our command – it shall be so.

So if you want peace, imagine it. This thought will create a feeling to which you can subscribe words and even name your true and original nature. Over and over again, imagine the peace you desire. Don't look upon it like looking at a picture, because it will manifest as beautiful scenes, like pictures, in which you will be able to gaze upon others in their lives experiencing peace, but it will still be far off for you. Instead, feel it. See, taste, and know it as real and possible right now and happening to you. Not like a movie or picture, you are watching, but something you are experiencing. What does peace smell like? What is around you when there is peace? What does it feel like? What does it taste like? How do you breathe and smile when you are at peace? Embrace and experience these things through all of your senses at the same time you are exploring it in your imagination. This energy will vibrate around you and draw you to peaceful situations—situations in which to choose and experience peace. Practice this repeatedly so you can realize that you can overcome any situation and create new and better-desired states. Make the unknown known to you so that you can have it.

People who know success and identify with it can recreate it anytime. That is why you will find individuals that have gone through things, lost everything and yet they are able to get right back up. They do not identify with the down times or the loss, they identify with the success and the move forward. It is their belief that they are a creator and can recreate anything—even that which appears lost. Truth is, in actuality, nothing is ever lost, and nothing is ever dead.

Many subconsciously know this to be true. You will see business people close one door and open another. Shut down one business and start another. A person with a belief system that they are a creator and can create or recreate anything, will always end up on their feet, no matter what the storm may look like in their life. They know success. They know it intimately. They have experienced it at every level of their being, with every sense they have in spite of the down moments. They know how to create it from inside (heaven) and manifest out (into the earth).

Know

How do you get to know something? By spending time with it. My Aunt Joyce would always correct us when, as children, we would say we knew someone. She would say, "No, you don't know them, you only know of them. To know someone is to be in relationship with him or her and to experience them on an intimate level. You, my child, only know of, you have not come to know anyone just yet." If you take a step back, you would find this to be true in your own life. You really do not know many things or people, you only know of.

My father would also share his wisdom that "You don't know anyone until you have seen them angry and watched how they fight. That will tell you everything you need to know, because anyone can be anybody if the stage is just right, but let things heat up, and the mask will come off." So wise and true! In order to know a relationship has to be established. Time has to be invested and familiarity and conditions have to be tested. Knowing is being in relationship with someone or something beyond causal knowledge. Knowing is to experience so that knowledge is obtained. There is a depth of actuality that comes with knowing.

You will know success when you can reach it, hold on to it, and believe in it even after and during failures. When you know and define yourself as success and do not define yourself by the failings, then life will always swing or shift you back into alignment with who you know yourself to be. Life will align itself with the "I am" statement you name yourself. i.e. – I Am success, I am love, I am blessed, I am favored, I am excellence, I am wise, I am....

Naming, seeing and defining is choosing. Defining by naming is believing in action. You will know success when you can image it as possible and for you, and imagine the work that comes with it as applicable to you. When you can taste it, and believe in it even when the world names you contrary and hopes for your demise, believe you are still named success and manifest in that nature. It is only what you believe that matters (materializes) in experience.

Let us be clear, just because you think good thoughts does not mean you will never experience the happenings of life. All things are common to man by consequence of life. Without the happenings of life, you cannot utilize your power and test the unlimited possibility of who you are. Your thoughts, your awareness and your belief can overcome, create, and recreate beyond any situations or circumstances. This is important, because many of life's happenings are occurring or projecting toward outside of our control. We are not the only players in the game of life, just the main player in the game of our lives. If we master controlling our own belief system of thoughts, we can experience the power to balance our lives and not be pulled in and remain dragged down by the thoughts or belief systems of others.

You must stay focused on you and not others. Know yourself. This is your call to action, KNOW YOURSELF. This journey is not about anyone or anything else. It is only about coming to know YOU, because when you know yourself, you will come to know God. If you come to know God, you come to know just how to love yourself. You must learn to love yourself enough to allow the greatest vision of yourself to manifest.

To be in relationship with your vision you must know it from a place of love of self. You have to spend time with it, test it, nurture it, try it, believe in it and wear its nature. You have to come into knowing. Experience how the vision of you feels, sounds, and tastes in your imagination so that you may know it without limitations. When you can't tell your vision from yourself and you from your vision, then you are in the knowing realm of your desire in which you and the Father are truly ONE. There is a oneness that must occur between you, God and the unadulterated vision of possibilities of you. From this harmony born of love, you can create with intention and clarity. Know and see your vision plainly, so you can create with distinction and clear direction.

Experience There

Experience is so powerful that it can limit you or release you. It can help you or hinder you. No matter what, you must make a choice within or beyond your experience that is in line with your own hopes and dreams. If you make a choice in and defined by experience and not in line with your vision and greatest self, you are choosing to experience the consequence of right now and delay your progress to the place over where you desire to go. Experiences and upheavals should not dictate your path or the journey. They are meant to be passed through and stepped over. Never a resting place to set up camp.

Experience is to serve as feedback, a directional suggestion that brings awareness of your opportunity to choose who you will be and who you are. Your vision and voice should speak from the vision you hold within. Not the one you have based on experiences you had or the lies others told you. It should come from within you. From that sacred place that holds all truths established prior to when you were placed in your mother's womb or contaminated by the hands of man and the hands of your own fractured self-worth.

This is why it is important to know who you are and have a true, clear and uncorrupted vision of yourself so you can also see your path clear. This is the only way you will know who you are and where you are going. Otherwise, you will travel any road trying to get somewhere you are not sure you should be going in the first place. All blessings and destinies are connected to a place. That is why you must always move forward in life and never look back. Your destiny is connected to a physical place, a place in your mind, a place in your spirit, a place in your career, or a place in your growth now and before you. Everything behind you is gone. If you keep the past with you today, it tethers you to yesterday, preventing you from moving into tomorrow with a full sensibility. You are trying to get "there" and not stay here or go backwards. Experience is often a hook that prevents or slows your progress to that place you call "there". That is why you often have to forsake it, in general, and scrub through the feedback it offers.

All the things you desire are manifested before you, but you must move forward to connect and receive them. They are manifested in that place called there. Here is the place you create, but there is where you will receive manifestation. Therefore, you must go there. Whenever and wherever Spirit is leading, you must go. You must always try to get there and never give up or settle here. Defy experiences and limited teachings. For behind the door less traveled through, there is a great path with less foot traction and congestion. It may not be as flat and smooth as the paths most traveled, but it will get you there in the uniqueness that is suited for you. This less-traveled path will create uniqueness in your experiences that will defy all previous thoughts and help solidify a new belief system that will usher in even more greatness that defies the limitation of your mind's belief system conjured by experience of life and man. It will take you away and around the plateaus for you to discover the tops of mountains untraveled. It is a path in which you discover yourself in relationship to Spirit. In relationship truth. A place that is not contaminated. A place in which new, more trustworthy experiences build new belief systems. Belief systems that lift you up to places not even your mind could have imagined on its own. Your specific purpose becomes clearer as you travel your unique path.

It is important to realize that the thoughts of your experiences that have created your reality today are the same things that limit your ability to move forward. But what is great about the experiences and thoughts of yesterday and the manifestation of today, is that we can look back and prove that the law of sowing and reaping, thought into manifestation is real and has shown itself in reality. What has or had our attention has or had our life. If we are honest, we can see that our present today is a manifestation of our thoughts and belief systems from yesterday. When you are creating today for a manifestation tomorrow be mindful of what you are thinking. You must disconnect from the past and all you thought and experienced yesterday, be presently conscious of a new thought today so you do not contaminate your creation that you will experience tomorrow. Don't run from yesterday, create a new day. Don't fight your past; embrace it as a map to navigate tomorrow. Everything has purpose, but not everything has permanency. Receive the feedback, release it according to its expiration date.

Law of First Thought

If we continue to focus on the reality of situations yesterday or even today, those things and the energy from those things will continue to hold our lives stagnant in the spirit of what was. We will continue to create and manifest yesterday from today into tomorrow. So STOP LOOKING BACK!! Now if the things you are looking upon are great thoughts and things like love and joy. That is great. But even that vision should be bigger and better for tomorrow. It should not have you tethered to someone who is gone. It should not be a comparison as if yesterday held the best days of your life. Build upon good for better. No looking back!

If we are not enjoying what is being created, we must change our focus to something else. Change the thoughts, focus and feelings, and the creation we manifest will as well. Stop comparing. Just create. It starts with our thoughts. The way to change a thought that is usually based on experience is through the creation of a new experience, to create new thoughts. This can happen in your mind through meditation and imagination. God sits in the secret place of your imagination, waiting for you to co-create with Him that which you desire to bring forth from heaven of the imagination into the earth of manifestation. The experience imagined creates a new thought and intention to create from.

In this place of imagination. You can command God's hand to bring about your heart's greatest desire. In this place, you can experience and create whatever you desire and receive it as reality and truth, and the universe will be in agreement with you for activation of manifestation.

Make sure the failings of yesterday are not allowed in the secret place. Remember to close out that which you do not desire when you create a new experience in your mind. See and feel this experience in your imagination and allow it to become real to you. So real that you can feel it with your physical senses, and the mood in your body shifts.

God speaks in scripture that we should meditate on these things that are true, noble, just, pure, lovely and of good report (Philippians 4:8) day and night. To see/declare the end from the beginning (Isaiah 46:10) and speak those things that be not as though they are (Romans 4:17), speaking those things into existence. It is a way to create and experience the feeling of those things that have not yet happened but we desire to manifest. Your creation in imagination is actually connecting to that which is already created. You are meditating, seeing and speaking to activate that which already is in Spirit to respond to your imaging of it in your imagination. This is your calling it off the shelf of abundance into your life. You are calling the things and feelings back into your and its remembrance. Remembering that you should and shall be one with one another. You are claiming that your desire is a part of you and must be experienced. That is why the experiencing in your imagination is important. This is where you touch and buy that which is intangible with your intangible power and sense of value and pull it into your experience. You are operating in your first nature of spirit and shifting the human nature to its secondary place. You thought and then vibrationally shifted to manifest in a human form from your original spirit form. You create in the same manner for the things you desire on your path. Spirit into matter. You have to go through the steps because it puts you at one vibrationally and spiritually. Remember that you cannot have what you have not known and you cannot know what you are not already. The experience in mind, body and soul is that important in creation. It brings things into knowing. If you have not had it in the earth yet, all you have to do is know it in spirit to be obtained in the earth. You are becoming one with that which you are to manifest.

Can You Feel It

You cannot always create or recreate an experience in reality. Meaning, you cannot recreate your experience when initially being asked to be married, or when you found out you were pregnant, won the lottery or got the promotion. The initial shock, angst, joy and excitement are impossible to recreate. It was an organic experience in consequence to the shock, as things became known in which you realized your dream just manifested before you. Even if you did try to recreate it, it would feel like a forced insincere reproduction. There would be no deep durable impact. False transient experiences are not as impactful as authentic ones.

One reason is that there is not an overload of the senses and mind simultaneously that weakens the conscious mind. The logical part of the mind is strong and rationalizes almost everything in accordance to what it already knows. When the conscious logical part of the mind is overloaded, it is weakened and the subconscious mind is empowered to operate freely and unguarded. This allows emotional and energetic changes to the subconscious in which the inconceivable can become conceivable enough at a depth of self to make a significant change in the mind. This shift within the mind can impact the overall belief system of the person having the experience. The shift in the mind causes a shift in behavior.

Behavior is a result of thought and feeling. Even if you change an outward behavior, eventually the behavior will fall back in line with the thoughts and feelings you hold because your true thoughts and feelings are more powerful energies than one's you have no real attachment. There is no real attachment to facades, so they don't actually utilize your energy or attention beyond the moment to survive. For a change in behavior to occur, you must have a solid shift in relation to a feeling experience along with a shift in thought. The feeling has to be felt to the core of you.. A feeling so intense, it shifts the core of who you are from inside out.

When you are able to capture the authentic feeling, you can then speak a new word or definition within you to align yourself with that abundant feeling. From the feeling and thought, you can create what you desire. However, make sure you are not in want when you create, but operating in desire and belief of what is known as possible. Remember that you are drawing near to and through you what already is. You desire what you know and what is already yours. Not something that is not of or for you. That is want. Want by definition is a state of poverty, famine, hunger, need, and lack. Want is a contradiction of abundance. You are not trying to get what you want. You must establish a state in which you are coming to know what you desire. You come into the awareness of what is, not what you do not have. Those are two different states of being.

In creation you want to embrace and increase the vibrational feeling of what and who you are. This is to bring about what you desire into manifestation in your life that is equal to that same vibrational feeling. If the feeling is want, then you create more want. If the feeling is abundance, you create more abundance. Whether the word you speak in the midst of the feeling is - I am peace, I am joy, I am wealth, I am free, I am love, I receive love freely, I receive new opportunities, etc. This word with the feeling is who you are. You get to name yourself and give yourself your nature. In the process of creation, you are utilizing, connecting and accepting this truth in spiritual experience and vibration. When you are clear on this aspect, then you set the stage for accurate manifestation.

The feeling you create is a general feeling. Do not be so specific. Being specific in qualifiers like things or people limit creation. No one thing, person or place should hold your joy, love, peace, abundance or anything else. It is the general feeling that you must understand your desire is held in. The things and people are just manifestations from the feeling. Not the other way around. So grasp the feeling of abundance and mimic the idea that you already are and already have the desired feeling of abundance in your imagination. When you focus on the feeling, the thoughts of things and people may come, but hold on to the feeling. Reason is that the feeling is the actual element of creation of the things and people. In the general feeling you exhibit, the thoughts of the things and individuals that contribute to this feeling.

As you feel and speak to yourself in your mind, the feeling married with your word will cause an intensification of the energy within you and around you, almost as if it is overwhelming you into a climax. Just continue to breathe it in for a few minutes to the point where you don't have to recreate the energy, thought, word, or feeling, but you could disconnect from the moment and go back to it in your mind when you need to because it becomes an intangible tangible place of refuge and creation. A quantifiable atmosphere you can touch, feel, and see all around you in your imagination. It is so real that when the other thoughts come to distract you, you will not look to the left or right. You will stay cleaved to your vision because you will know with great clarity within you who you are and what you do desire.

From this new thought settled within you, you give the universe a new vision to manifest and a palpable established environment to work in and through with you. The place called there will manifest into a here and now moment to be walked and lived in. Using this power within you, you can begin to sit on the throne of your own life and not be driven

PART II – LAW

In the Beginning

"In the beginning was the word and the word was with God and the word was God" (John 1:1). This one line tells us all we need to know about who we are and what power we hold. It explains the grandness and expansiveness of who we are. The remainder of the story of creation illustrates to us how we do and can create intuitively and explicitly.

In understanding the creation story, we also come to understand that all things created have a beginning. A beginning defined by a word, born out of a thought. This Word of God was manifested out of a thought. There was thought held by the Creator in which a word was then formed. The word given to anything is the power and defined nature given to that thing based on the thought that qualifies its existence. That is why the power of our word is emphasized in almost all Holy Scriptures. The word is the beginning of all things created. Your word is the god power of your creation. A word spoken is always in authority and one with the life, existence and resulting creation of he who speaks the word.

There is no separation between your word and your creation. There is no separation between God and his spoken creation. Just as scripture states that I and the Father Are One (John 10:30), I am also one with my word and the word of the Creator with whom I am aligned. Am or Are means to remain, stand, stay, co-exist, survive, be alive, be present, be real, occur, transpire, ensue, take place and come to pass. When we "are" one or "am" one these are the definitions to which we subscribe.

Remember that the word is God and the word is with God and from the beginning was the word. Illustrating there is no separation between the speaker of a word and the word. Henceforth, understand that there is no separation between you and the Father, who is your Creator that spoke you into being. There is no separation from the creator and the created. Therefore, there is no separation between the spoken and the manifested. You, in the likeness of that which has begotten you by thinking and speaking of you, operate in the same manner. There is no separation between you and your word. Your word is, with and of, you and in the likeness and image of you.

Thoughts, beliefs, and your words are all creating the world you have and will experience. They are the gods creating the future to behold. They are also a mirror of the thoughts you hold of yourself yesterday and today. In Genesis of the Bible, we are given insight into creation.

We are constantly in a struggle to figure life out, but in the beginning before anything was created, a format was laid out for us. Everything that was to come and everything that is, has and does follow the pattern of creation and manifestation. It has all been laid out for us. We have been conditioned not to trust it. We are often raised to look outside at the tangible and not within at the intangible.

We have already come to understand that creation has a process. You first have the thought that conjures a feeling, and then you generate and speak the word. The feeling furnishes a nature that presents clarity of a word to be uttered. When a word is spoken, it solidifies the image held by the creator. It bestows a nature, a symbol, a purpose, direction and power to manifest. From here, the cycle of creation moves in full action toward the last step of manifestation. When the thought moves from vision to word, it connects with the power of God in you to manifest.

When this revelation came to me, I took some time, looked back over my life, and replayed many stories and experiences. I read and analyzed my own life. I questioned myself. I questioned God, as well as what I thought I knew and believed of God, angels and the universe. I meditated. I wondered. I watched. I accepted. I experimented. I realized that everything we all do, say, and believe is not only based on a word, but that the word is based on an original thought we hold within us. If we are honest, our lives truly do reflect what it is we think, feel and say. We are experiencing, in some form or fashion, what we think and speak. Our life is our creation.

We often hear that we must speak positively. In this aspect, we are focused on the words we speak. However, we are missing a crucial part of the creation process. We are forgetting to ask and evaluate our thoughts and the energy we feed ourselves. The thoughts we hold are essential to our lives. They reveal the truth of what we believe despite the words we speak in the company of others. What are we saying to ourselves? What are we saying behind closed doors?

We cannot lie to our own mind or spirit. Because the word and its creator are one, the word is in the image and likeness of the heart, mind and spirit of the creator. So maybe we should not look so much at the words we say, but that which forms and speaks the word. If we can change our thoughts, we can change our personal world and resulting experiences.

Become Aware

We have been blind to the keys to unlock the potential of our lives. Blind to its operational process and power. Blind to the fact that we are creators with the inherent power to make, break, create and recreate our lives and experiences. Creation is actually an automatic process for us. We do it every day without realizing it. We are constantly in the process of creation. We are just not conscious of it. We have been conditioned to be unconscious of the process and view the process of creation as being outside of ourselves. As if we are victims with no power to yield. We must become aware of our power to use it effectively.

If we take a moment and realize how we have already been misusing our power, we will see how to make the necessary thought changes to make this power work for us and what this power can do. From this awareness, we can create with intention and intensity by speaking our true intention that is aligned with our beliefs into manifestation.

Imagine that just one thought can change your life. Just one thought can change the language and feeling of your life. Change in this one area can manifest an entirely different experience. It is that simple and yet, that serious of a power we have.

Who would have thought the thoughts are the seeds connected to every experience and harvest in our life? Have you ever taken a moment to analyze your thoughts?

I Am Like God

Made in his image, made in his imagination.

Your imagination is the place where the image that I am the nation operates. There is a knowing in your imagination that I am all things, and all things exist, operate, and are one with me. This is the Christ-consciousness in which we do not find it robbery to be equal with God, but necessary.

God thought all of creation into being. We are all a thought. All that we know, all that is tangible is a manifestation of thought. When God thought, an image was formed in the mind. From the image came a word. This word gave voice, name and nature to the thought. God's belief and attention on his thought gave the thought the energy necessary to form from the intangible into a tangible matter. God saw creation before it was manifested. He looked upon the image, and meditated on the feeling of the images' existence. He felt and believed that the image he created was a good thing. He rested in the feeling of the good He created. When he spoke the word of his creation, He spoke the word as if the creation was formed. He did not speak the process, the steps or the beginning stage of anything. He spoke it and named it in the fullness of its possibility. He named all things in its complete wholeness, from the beginning. Nothing was named according to its process, beginning, transitioning or evolution. All things were named according to its nature of goodness, completion and sufficiency.

Because thought is created in the mind, it does not manifest in formation until after the spirit rests in what is thought, spoken, seen or believed. This is the process. The process God demonstrated. The process we also have the ability to use. The process we actually use every second of every day without being aware. That is just how powerful belief and words are. Your mind is the womb of conception for your life. Words bound to this conception process, married with belief, originate material production.

The next step to recognize in the process of creation demonstrated for us is that there was never another thought God thought when He operated in this process of creation. He maintained a clear vision. This vision consisted of clarity visually perceived, pureness in energy attained and harmony relating name and nature. All of this was formed fully in His imagination, agreed upon within His entire being and experienced at the same time through His senses.

We are a concept materialized by the imagination of our Creator and in the likeness of his being. As a matter of fact, God says that He is not a man that He should lie or change His mind. By not changing His mind, He has the integrity of His mind and heart and spirit, therefore His creation is intentional and reflective of Him. He speaks surely what He desires and what is born of His own imagination and nature. What He says and what He thinks, He is. The standard of operation God abides by has established the law that He operates out of. It is the law of creation, the law that what is spoken will manifest. This is true also for us: we are replicas. Therefore, what we sow in thought or belief is reaped in manifestation. That manifestation is a harvest created out of the first and original thoughts of our belief system. The law of first thought is the law of creation, the law of manifestation.

God has let us in on the secret that being double-minded is destructive, because two opposing thoughts cannot stand. They cancel each other out. That is not creation. That is destruction. The integrity of the thought and word brings about creation that is of the primary premeditated nature of the creator. That is why you must watch your thoughts, your own energy, and your emotions when thinking and speaking, because your creation is a reflection of your own nature at the moment creation occurs. You will, by law, create an incarnation of your imagination in line with and affected by the essence of your likeness. You will sow a seed that looks and feels like you. All seeds bring forth some form of a harvest. It is the law.

I Am the Truth and the Light

So what is law? God is law. God is process, creation, and the created. There is nothing He is not, and yet, He is not any one thing. Just as we are not just one thing. We are many things, and yet none of these things we perceive. We are constantly changing, evolving, manifesting and destroying the concepts and experiences of our own lives. Man is always in the process of manifesting out of the abundance of all that is possible. Being what was and yet creating what is to come. This is all happening first in the mind. Being, changing, discovering, creating. Life itself is always happening first in the mind. Therefore, what we put, or allow, in the mind will determine the outcome of our lives.

So when it is time to make a change, we realize that it must start with our thoughts. God, the mind, which is the creation machine, does not need changing. They both operate perfectly according to the law. It is our thoughts that create our belief system about ourselves, others, and our place in life that has to change for change in life experience to take place. The mind itself is faultless in its operation. It cannot do anything other than what it has been programmed to do. Its output is based on the input into this system. The reservoir of thoughts put in the system of your mind is usually from your overall belief system. Therefore, to change the output, you must change the mind's input, your belief system.

The belief system writes the law of life's operation that governs within your mind. To change your mind's output, you must change the laws it operates from. When you change your beliefs, you change the thoughts formed from the belief that create more laws and thoughts in line with the new belief. You must be transformed by the renewing of your mind. When you change the mind's thoughts, your life will follow.

What Is Law

What is law? According to Merriam's Dictionary, law is defined as "a rule or order that is advisable or obligatory to observe, a rule of construction or procedure, a department of knowledge."

The Oxford definition of law says that it is "the system of rules, which a particular country or community recognizes as regulating the actions of its members, a rule defining correct procedure or behavior, and a statement of fact deduced from observation to the effect that a particular natural or scientific phenomenon always occurs if certain conditions are present." It regulates actions and it defines intentional procedure or behavior. It is a fact found to be true through experience and routinely produces a result in accordance.

Recognize that the intention of the law is to define and regulate actions, procedures and behaviors. As we know law, we know that law can be corrupted, misused and incorrect procedures can occur. Why? Because law does not define itself by good or bad, right or wrong, but intention. The nature of the intention is important when you work within the law, because the law itself will regulate, produce and influence process, behavior and result. The law is good--it is what we put in the law and how we use the law and what we do with the law that corrupts. That is why we must be cognizant of law in order to know how to use it for our intended good, appropriately.

If we take this same understanding into a spiritual context, we will go deeper into the depths of where our real existence and power lies. According to spiritual law of the mind, our thoughts regulate our thinking and actions and ensure certain conditions and outcomes. Our mind and our spirit are one. The personality or persona and its experience are conditional consequences of how regulated or unregulated we adhere to and master the law. As well as, what you write into law of your mind.

Let's look back again at the process of the mind in the understanding of law. The mind is the Father, the command center, of you. You are one with this Father. You are putting in the thoughts that reflect who you are in the mind. In the mind is where your thoughts that reflect you become one with the Father. There is no separation between you and your thoughts. You are one.

How does this work in your mind's process? Well, you are a trinity of existence, a trinality--a replication of the trinity. The father (the mind) is the law that dictates, regulates, defines, creates, and produces. It regulates and determines outcomes and productivity. The mind is not the belief system. The belief system consists of thoughts from experience and given knowledge. They are thoughts you give power to make laws within the mind's legal system. It impacts what you will or will not receive or create with the Father in mind. It puts in limits or removes them. It opens itself to options and opportunities or turns its back on open doors presented by the mind. Many times these thoughts of the belief system are contradictory to the truths of the Father and or your innate spiritual truth and nature. Recognize that you are in the center of it all.

The law is a powerful tool, but also an informing mechanism. The law maintains order, but also it informs. It informs us of the foundation of thought, precedence, history, experience, common belief, culture, and hope. It exposes weaknesses and builds strengths. The law never fails in general application and is trustworthy to do what it has been designed to do. If used properly, it will do as it has been established to do for the higher good. If used inappropriately or unconsciously, it will still bring about the inappropriate, unconscious or routinely normal outcomes.

Knowledge of the law empowers us and informs us of our rights, expectations, power and responsibilities. It assists us in knowing who we are in the overall system in which we are governed. It lets us know what to expect and what not to expect. It gives us the power to create. It gives us the power to change. No more guessing is necessary when you understand the law, because the law is explicit in its operation. You only have to operate within the law to receive its promised outcome.

Remember that the outcome and the law are for and about you. Not others. You cannot have an expectation on others to live, abide by or adopt your law or nature. You are governing yourself in order to assure your own life and its resulting experiences and outcomes. This is about your peace, joy, prosperity, success and the like. Whatever flows out from you into the world and is received and appreciated by others of like mind or of appreciative spirits is just the consequence of the energy and nature of authenticity you bring. This walk is about you. Changing, conforming, shining or dimming for other people, other thoughts or acceptance allows your power to be placed in the hands of man and their personality and out of the hands of your trinality.

Original Thought

Your first thought is the thought that is leading this endeavor train. It is the foundation of all other thoughts. It is what you are directed by, advised from, and operating within. It is your department of knowledge. Your first thought is the rule of construction on which you live. It informs with the knowledge it holds on the processes and procedures of your life. Everything in your life is hinged on your original first thought.

You create, believe, and experience out of your original thought. The original thought you hold and live by is usually a subconscious thought, one that was created from an experience or word spoken to you that you held within you. This experience created a thought, which created a seed of a word that was planted in your unconscious mind. The thought created was cultivated over time and has grown to such a degree that the only way it can be changed is if a more powerful thought or belief is given and accepted. The new thought then takes the power and energy away from the old thought and cultivates the new one.

We have many thoughts. Each thought is built upon another. A thought of unworthiness may be built upon a thought my parents were never there, the school did not care, men always abuse me, etc. The opposite would occur for worthiness. I am worthy, my parents informed me as such, I have many accolades, I win all the time, etc.

The culmination of many thoughts creates a belief system by which you live. All of these thoughts make up the law of your being. Your belief system is who you are, who you were, and who you will be. It is the same yesterday, today, and tomorrow unless you change it with new thoughts and new knowledge, which will cause a transformation by the renewing of your mind and subsequent thoughts.

Whatever the belief, the original thought is the one that has established the law of your life's operation and experiences. Thoughts and experiences, by law, come to acknowledge, increase, expand, support and magnify the original thought you hold because you as the creator of it. They want to support you in your belief and efforts of who you are. Because the universe loves you so much to support you in this life experience it keeps giving you more of what you ask and giving you more of whom you say you are. It only wants to please you by answering your call. It piles on more and more because you keep asking for the same thing and feeling the same way. Until you change your mind of who you are, you cannot put in a different order in your life. Your mind does not want to contradict you in that manner.

Lord's Prayer

When Jesus gave the Lord's Prayer it was not just a prayer instructing us on what to say, but how to once again be a part of the creative process with intention. It was an awakening to the truth of the law in which we live, breathe, and have our true being. The Lord's Prayer begins with calling oneself into awareness and activation. When we pray, we are calling to manifest that which is in heaven into the earth. In other words, we are activating by calling and coming into awareness, that which is in the mind, into matter manifestation and experience. Heaven is the creative imagination of your mind. The kingdom is your creation created in the mind's imagination, with the power of the Father.

The rest of the prayer is how to align yourself in gratitude, forgiveness, peace, and oneness with the Father. This intentional alignment is important because when you connect with the Father, this connection brings about a manifestation in the full likeness of your mind (heaven) into physical manifestation (earth). Since who you are spiritually, mentally and emotionally will be manifested in your life, it is important that when you are operating in creation, that you do it without judgment. It is necessary to release the baggage of other things, thoughts, people, relationships and ideals because those trespasses will contaminate you and your life. Bringing in negative energy mars creation made with the Father.

Once again we are given keys to unlock our ability to operate on our behalf. Here Christ is giving us guidelines on how to bring about clear, profitable and aware creation and manifestation. We are being educated on how to create with clarity and integrity in our thoughts, words and feelings. The mind and our senses all play a part in creation.

Our mind is the place dreams are made or destroyed. Any tampering or tainting will manifest in our creation and life experiences. To override this occurrence, we must understand how we work... Knowing how we function further relieves us from the victim concepts and the wondering if God likes me better than my neighbor or vice versa. This brings you back into your right mind of power. It is not your outward deeds as much as your inward deeds that bring about your heart's desire. No matter what you have or have not done, said, lived, or what your life looks like, you and the Father are one! Through this truth, you have the power to create or recreate your life to be anything you desire. You have the power. Any thought you have that distorts this truth distorts your life and limits your ability to create the greatness that you are intended to be.

Meditate on These Things

Scripture states that, "Finally, brethren, whatsoever things are true, whatsoever things are honest, whatsoever things are just, whatsoever things are pure, whatsoever things are lovely, whatsoever things are of good report; if there be any virtue, and if there be any praise, think on these things," (Phil. 4:8, KJV).

Part III – Speak Co-Creator

Meditation is important, because who you are in the moment will impact the seed you sow in your imagination and, therefore, the harvest. Make your mind a place of fertile and positive soil to receive the fruit you desire. "Then the serpent said to the woman, 'You will not surely die. For God knows that in the day you eat of it your eyes will be opened, and you will be like God, knowing good and evil,' " (Gen. 3:4–5, NKJV).

In the beginning, you knew that you were not just like God, but that you were (and are) God. The taking of a body did not separate you from this oneness. It is an illusion that many of us have bought into, just as Adam and Eve demonstrated in the story above. The only reason Eve would think she needed to be like God is because she was allowed to think a thought of herself as less than equal with God. The question posed to her by the serpent caused her to doubt her own greatness, power and established authority. Philippians 2:6 (KJV) says "who, being in the form of God, thought it not robbery to be equal with God."

To be Christ-like is to think and be as Christ. Christ operated and saw through a consciousness much higher than most of us attempt to achieve. Not because we cannot, we just choose not to partake and accept the responsibility of this higher consciousness. We fail to do the necessary work to reawaken and rise from the dead of our being into the light of our greatness. To think and be as Christ would is to believe that you are in the form of God, and you no longer think it is robbery to be equal with God. You may not be the God of the Universe all by yourself, but you are the god of your universe, empowered by the God, and as a part of such, you are a creator of all that is in your nation (out of your imagination) and the universe of which you are a part. You are that powerful. There is no power that you lack, except for what you believe to be missing. You must take responsibility for this power if you desire change. Using meditation directs the power of creation.

The conversation Eve had with the serpent was a twist on a number of truths in which seeds were planted to change the first thought of oneness Eve should have known to be true. In the story, if the serpent was able to change her mind and her thoughts about herself and her God, which is what he did, then he could change her word, her behavior, and then change the outward projection of her life.

Let's be clear in the Adam and Eve story. It is important to have clarity because it affects your belief in your own power. No enemy. No otherness. Nothing has any power other than the power you give it. In this story, there were only questions presented, no power revealed or yielded over anyone. In almost all situations there is an illusion of an imbalance of power or a perceived presence of power. Without evidence it is only implied or assumed. Questions are meant to bring clarity; however, they can also bring about uncertainty, doubt, and confusion when you are not secure and sure of yourself. That is what occurred in this story.

The only way anyone or anything can convince you to give them power is by planting seeds that cause you to question yourself, in your mind, that cause a distortion of your current belief system. Remember, all seeds sown in your mind's soil bring a harvest. If you accept another's seed about you, it is your harvest now to reckon with.

Your mind is the most powerful and most vulnerable thing you possess. You must protect it, direct it and master the power of it by thinking and knowing who you are. If anything or anyone can change your thought and influence your belief, they can change how you behave and what you will or won't say or create on your behalf. That is what makes television, politics, and religion so powerful. They are going out of their way to try to influence your belief system. Hard at work attempting to change your mind to line up with their belief, doctrine, or marketing ploy. With the intention to affect your behavior for you to buy their product, follow them, watch their shows, vote for their idea, or give them your power and money.

It is up to you to decide if this alignment is beneficial or detrimental. That is why you must always be cognizant of your power and have a firm grasp of it in your own hand. Anything received from another should be discriminately questioned and discerned. Ask a question of the question to bring clarity for you.

The same way thoughts and words can change your beliefs and help you, it can hinder you and can be used to manipulate you, which is why you should always question the thoughts you have or thoughts others present to you. Does this bring me life or death? Is what I am currently doing and believing bringing me the good I desire, or will a change in the way I think open a door that is better for me than where I am? Who benefits from this the most, the person telling me this or myself? Is this about me, them, or something greater? Why are they telling me this? How has this thought worked for them and others like me? Does it sound or feel true to me? Questions are your friends. Lack of answers and self-doubt make you vulnerable. However, lack and doubt of answers can be beneficial by bringing you feedback for clarity and direction. Never fear questions. Ask more questions until the answers come, and you know who you are and who you are not. Meditate in clarity and assurance.

Sow and Receive

You ever heard the saying, what you put out comes back to you? What you believe in magnifies. The laws you create for others become law for you as well. It all comes back to you. You usually make rules and laws for and about others because of what you think about you. In essence, you create laws with you in mind every time. It is usually not about others, but it is always about you.

Your life will reflect the harvest received from what you have sown in thought. You may ask, "How did I sow so much pain to receive so much pain?" It may not have been pain you sowed. It may have been complacency you sowed. Remember that the feeling and thought can often be general, but will bring about specific experiences in line with the overall feeling and thought held. That is why I have expressed the importance of clarity.

Using our power to speak things we do not desire like... "I am sad", "I am lost", "I am lonely", "I never get what I want", and "I am always trying", has consequences. Whatever you say, you receive. The more you say it, the more of it you receive. The more energy you give it, the greater the return. If you call yourself a victim you receive more victimization in line with the nature you named and chose to speak over your life. If you have a belief that bad things always happen to you, it is due to you seeing that as your nature. It is the seed you sow unconsciously that returns to you as a harvest. I hear some responding as they read, that they say it because it is their reality. I say to you, that you had an experience in which you then defined yourself by. Once you took on the definition of the experience and laid down your original nature in line with the Father in you, life gave you experiences in line with the definition you held. You, aware of this truth now, have the power to re-define.

Seed

If your seed is contaminated with the experiences of yesterday, the harvest will reflect this contamination. If your pain, the neglect from your parents, the abuse of your ex, your inability to achieve in organized educational systems as a child, and all of those other things have you doubting yourself, (self-sabotage) stopping you, then your seed will reflect this. You cannot sow a seed that does not have your fingerprint on it. Your seed is a reflection of the truth of you. To change the harvest, change your thought. Don't try to overcome yesterday or disprove it. Be transformed with a new thought of yourself that you are good, you are a survivor, you are a conqueror, you are blessed, you are love, you are lovable, you are grateful, you are forgiven as you forgive yourself and others, and you are free. From this place of whole truth, healing, and freedom, know that you are not limited and that all things truly are possible for you. For in the place of unlimited possibility lies the greatest existence of you. Sow energy and thoughts with the fingerprint of this greater and positive part of you, the higher you. The you that is one with the Father. Watch the harvest reflect this new nature of you.

Rid yourself of the past thoughts: what you wanted to tell somebody, what you are going to tell them when you see them, and all that jazz. Let it go! Bless it all, and bless them all. Try this: See the people and the drama you once toiled with regularly in your mind, standing before you as if they were all standing out on a table. Tell them and it "I bless you to be your greatest self for yourself and I let you all go. I forgive you, and I forgive myself for allowing you to stay here this long. I pray you find your peace, and I take my own peace back." Breathe deep, and as you let the air out of your lung, let them, let it all go, and watch how your breath blows it all from your mind's vision. Then lift up your head, close your eyes, and see the abundance of the universe. Now breathe and expand within the universal limitedness in your mind. Take your rightful place on the throne in the vastness of your mind and redirect your attention from the lowly and the small to the abundance and the great "I am" to take your hand and create the masterpieces of your life. He has been waiting to intentionally create and manifest with you.

Speak a Thing

Therefore, when we say "I Am," we are confessing, allowing, acknowledging, and directing the universe to come into alignment with what we have stated and believe to be true, even if it is for the moment. We are sowing second, minute, and lifetime seeds. When you sow, the universe does not judge if it is a lie, a joke, a scheme, or a truth, because it does not judge. It only responds to your word in order to maintain your integrity in the universe and further its integrity of manifestation of your stated desire. The angels, principalities, energy, nothing has been formed to judge, only to respond on your behalf.

When Adam and Eve spoke that they were naked, lacking, in need, and separate, that is what they experienced—a separation in which nakedness and lack were created. God did not curse them or abandon them. He only agreed with their statement of themselves and told them what that new thought meant for them. They could not be in the land of abundance if the statement of "I am" is lack. That would be out of integrity. He asked them specifically, "Man, where are you?" They did not realize they were still in abundance, despite the many crazy thoughts, I am sure, flooded their heads. They stated, "We are here, and we are naked." Here where? In their mind, where they became aware of the other side of abundance, where judgment lives, and where evil has a face is where they were. They no longer trusted their own power or the perfection of their imperfections.

You cannot be in the midst of more than enough when your I Am statement is "I have not enough and am not enough." God did not punish Adam and Eve; He accepted what they said. He did not curse Adam and Eve; He gave them their stated desire out of the abundance of their heart that their thoughts created a new reality for them. Though they possessed the power to name every beast of the field and gave everything in the garden their corresponding nature by speaking the nature into being, Adam and Eve came into a new thought presented by a question that they were less than. They were in full operation in the oneness with God, their source, and they got confused. They had no wants, but took on the nature of want. They focused on the limitation of the flesh presented to them and disowned the expansiveness of their spirit. With fear taking over, they separated themselves from each other, their land of plenty and pleasure, as well as communing intimately with their God. They did this in their thoughts. This was not a physical separation, because the truth is, they were still in the midst of everything they thought they did not have any longer. The lack and separation was an illusion of the mind misguided by irrational thinking.

PART III -- SPEAK CO-CREATOR

Part III – Speak Co-Creator

Honesty Can Set You Free

There comes a time when we must be truly honest with ourselves about who we are and what we think of ourselves as well as others. Self-evaluation is a valuable mechanism. It is similar to the anti-virus software on your computer. The routine self-evaluation keeps you at optimum operation. If it can catch the virus or a hint of any potential problem in its initial stage, it can contain and remove it before it starts to destroy the operating system. It can guarantee another day of successful operation. When the computer is running slow and losing some of your documents, that is not the time for evaluation. You will end up having to conduct a total reboot. If you fail to do a deeper analysis and reboot of your operating system, the problem will not only persist, but you are in danger of a total crash and loss of everything you have worked on.

We are no different from a computer. We must do an evaluation on our mind to see if there are viruses or malware destroying our ability to operate at our optimum level. We must be honest about the contempt we hold, the anger we fester or suppress, the doubt, the hope, the misguided thoughts, contemplations, what we know, what we do not know, what we have failed to do, when we have given our all, tried our best, not exhausted all options, the fears we have, and the promises we hold within our hearts—especially the secret ones. No matter how secret you may think they are, they have power. No matter if you utter them or not, they maintain space in the mind of creation. Just like any clay in a potter's hand or on the potter's wheel, something shall be formed out of it. It may be an unconscious formation, but nonetheless, a formation shall manifest out of the hand of its creator. Whatever you hold in your mind, no matter how miniscule the thought or big the dream, something must manifest when it comes in contact with the power of belief in your mind.

Honesty about our thoughts and beliefs help to set us free. It empowers us. If we know what we are thinking and dealing with, we can overcome the thoughts and put our focus and power toward that which we truly desire. Stealing power from thoughts, feelings and consequences of life we do not desire can only happen if we are honestly aware of what we are thinking, feeling and dealing with. Truth is always the key to freedom. It may not always appear to be, because the truth can bring about as much pain as a lie at times, but a lie holds one in bondage. The truth allows you freedom and the removal of guilt and shame. A lie cannot. When you are honest about your thoughts, then and only then can they be released so as not to plague you. The plague, as long as it is in the secret place of your heart, grows and contaminates all aspects of you. Seeping into the veins and arteries of your life's existence, influencing everything you touch, breath and speak. It may start small and then slowly begin to kill and harm without your awareness until the damage is done, just as a lie. When you let the lies and unwanted viruses go, the other stuff it has manifested will also be released and removed out of your life as well.

This freedom helps you when you are operating in intentional creation. Remember that you are the only one that can limit love, light and the answer yes to your prayers. Your thoughts direct the hand of God. Your thoughts move the hand of creation into a box, overshadowed and tainted by your thoughts. Or you can free the hand to bring about what it holds for you. You are the director. You are the creator limiting or freeing your creation. God, the universe, the angels are all subjected to your will unless you submit to the greater will. Either is your choice. You are in control of choosing and directing. That is your gift of operation. Self-reflection utilized effectively is necessary to get the most from this gift. It is necessary so that you may free yourself and allow your intended, desired and gifted creation to soar beyond the limits of your mind and within the unlimited vastness of the Universal God power.

My Power to Speak Works for Me

If you attempt to use your power on another, you will not get a response, because your power is for the creation in your life. However, if a person is of one mind and one accord with you or accepting of your thought, then the two or more of you gathered together around this thought the same mind and on the same accord exude a greater energy force of creation (Matthew 18:20). This is an agreement of thought and not a forcing of belief. You cannot override another's thought or creation for them, only for your own self. Even if you think you are doing something to another, it's an illusion. The truth is, when a person changes their mind or belief system, it is because they have chosen to and created a new thought within themselves. Your life or your actions may cause someone to rethink things for themselves and change their mind about something, but it is they who will have to change their mind in order to change their life. They will have to choose differently in order to experience differently.

Even when we pray and think we are changing another, it is not us who changes them, nor our prayers. Our prayer offers opportunity for them to choose and see. Through the awareness they choose, an awakening then occurs. From this awareness, a new choice can be made. It is always their choice. If they do not choose, it will not happen. Your prayer shifts for revelation; but in the end, it is always the other person who must make the choice for themselves.

Another's imagination of creation is not in our hand. They always have a say and can hinder your word or thought, because your word, your power is for and about you only. No one else. So when you speak, you speak for and about yourself. When you speak an, you are establishing who or what you are I Am statement and what shall be for the benefit or detriment of yourself, even if it is toward another. Unless they accept the negative energy and thoughts you have for them, it will return to sit at your feet. All thoughts and energy return to the creator of the thought and energy unless accepted and taken on by another. Even then, the creator must reckon with its creation in some form or fashion.

When you speak a thing, you have already accepted it as true. Not for another, but in general, which means for you as well. Out of the mouth speaks the heart. You cannot lie to yourself. You can only agree or struggle with the truth, but you cannot lie to yourself or speak a truth not congruent or possible of you in line with your own belief. Whatever you say, the universe will align your life to reflect it. Therefore, if you do lie to yourself, know that the lie will attempt to be made true to keep you in integrity of self. The self-delusion is itself a delusion.

You desire your own integrity—integrity that lines up with your heart's desire and not the shadow of yourself. If you lie that you are sick for sympathy, then sickness for sympathy is what shall be given to you. Your "I-am" sick statement in which you give thought, feeling, and verbalization to is a seed that brings you a harvest—a harvest of integrity aligned with your word.

"Let the weak say I am strong and the poor say I am rich." (Joel 3:10) Why? Because you cannot hold true a lie or a contradiction in your spirit. You are a perfect creation. A being with integrity of name and nature. You can be what you say or say what you are or desire to be and become it. However, you cannot say one thing and be another. You have to stay or come into alignment to one or the other. Your life aligns with the thoughts and words you hold and speak of the creation you are or perceive yourself to be. Though you are perfect, if you say you are not, then what you say shall be. Your wish, your word, is your command. Command ye my hand sayeth the Lord (Isaiah 45:11). If you say you are weak, then weakness has to find a space within you to help you become that which you say and believe you are. If you continue to confess, believe, and feel a new truth, then the universe will have to shift to align with the truth you now speak. You create the nature within your imagination, name yourself "I am" that, and manifestation will follow in the image of its creator's word.

This is significant so that we may be able to recognize and separate our true thoughts and beliefs from those offered us from others. Many times we accept and take on thoughts of others without analyzing them. Therefore, commanding our lives in the direction others have for themselves or have for us. The directional command should come from within. We should never put another god before our God or our own god power. Only you hold the blueprint of your life created before you were placed in your mother's womb. Taking on thoughts contradictory to authenticity can stunt your soul's development and life's potential satisfaction. Make sure when offered new thoughts that you analyze the benefit or detriment to you. Do not take on thoughts of people because of where they live, what they look like, how convincing they sound, because they are important to us, because they are our parents, an elder, our friends, our lovers, church members, politicians or have money. Evaluate the resignation from within. Too many times we are hypnotized by the outside container of the thought holder and the energy and veracity of the messenger. Failing to analyze the thought offered and the benefit or hindrance that thought has on our lives and overall belief system can mean we just downloaded a virus-infected program, masquerading as good intention.

Whatever You Say Shall Be

The *I Am* statement is the most powerful statement there is. This statement defines, directs power, and manifests the unconscious thoughts we have of ourselves and others. The *I Am* statement is using the power of the tongue to create and form on your behalf. When using this power, there is no shield or protection other than the power itself to recreate or destroy the initial creation. There is direct connection between the power of creation and the power of the tongue. You are your own shield and sword, either defending or killing yourself. The greatest statement God spoke in revelation is "I Am That I Am." (Exodus 3:14). Meaning, there is nothing that I am not and all that is, I am. This is a statement of the unlimited and undefinable existence of that which cannot be explained with limited vocabulary and conceptualization. The limitlessness can only be experienced in the true nature of unlimited possibilities. Whatever you can think of, God, creation and imagination can conform, transform, and will take on that nature. Any and all things thought or spoken, *I Am*. Therefore, you, in the likeness and image of God, You Are also whatever you think, speak or believe.

When people of faith—any faith—speak of God, Allah, the Universe, the unnamable or whatever you may call Him/Her/It, they are speaking and professing what God is to them. They are speaking of their known experience in relationship to God's power or what they desire the nature of God to be for them. They may profess that He is a healer. What they are stating is that they are accepting the healing nature of God in order to receive that part of Him for themselves and their situation. At times they are hoping He is a healer or wish He proves them right or wrong because this is a new aspect of God they are coming to experience. They may have known him as a provider, but now they are coming to experiencing and know him in another way.

When individuals profess that which they know or believe is possible of God, this is faith in. Not actual faith, however. The individual is accepting the I Am unlimited possibility of the nature(s) of God. However, because we have not all experienced all aspects of God, it is often faith in the aspects we have not yet come to know. Knowing establishes the faith. Many times, we just hope and have faith in the possibilities unknown or new to us. For this to change to actual faith, we must come to accepting and believing and not hoping and speaking, because the belief of, from knowing, makes it so and not just possible. The "I Am that I Am" is what gives faith to humans that they can trust that if this power or nature has worked or been present in any one situation it is possible and available to operate on their behalf in all other situations in the same if not a great capacity. This takes the knowing through a specific experience away as a criteria knowing can be established by way of relationship. It makes it easier to speak with confidence that what you say and whatever aspect you need to operate on your behalf is possible to and for you.

When you know the creator, you know the creation in its likeness. You are the unlimited possibilities of God. You are the nature and manifestation of God, the power of God and all that God is and chooses not to be. So whatever nature you choose to take on, whatever you name yourself and know yourself to be, you are. There is nothing you cannot be. You can take on whatever nature and possibility you say, think and believe. That is why it is important that you are mindful of what you name yourself and the nature you take on in your thoughts, words and feelings. What you believe you say. What you say, you become. What you become, is what you believed.

Your Power Is Where You Say It Is

No one has more power than you when it comes to you. It may not appear that way at times. That is only because you have bought into the lie that we are not all created in God's image and, therefore, not all equal in capability and capacity. You have bought the lie that you are less, and—unconsciously, from this belief—you have submitted your power to another person, an entity, a principality, a degree, money, tangible power and systems of men or some other thing. You give your power away, because you believe that another person or something has the power to give or take away from you what is inherently yours. You believe that your lack of perceived outward power is evidence of a power transfer away or outside of you. This is not a real transfer of power, because we always have the power. It is never absent from us. Your belief that you do not hold the power yields the power dormant for you to use and makes it accessible to be utilized on another's behalf because you leave it vulnerable to others. Your belief that someone or something has power is what causes the power shift and gives another what appears to be the assumed power. Real power is your power of belief and power of choice. This is the universal gift.

Slaves, captured servants and colonized countries throughout history were freed not because of the great kindness of slave owners and colonizers, but because there were a few men and women who did not limit their ability to believe in freedom and to choose life in the face of death. They chose life, but accepted the possibility that death could bring freedom. They did not limit the vision to only one path. They opened the path to include all possibilities. It sounds crazy, but allowing the option of death to enter the picture of freedom, is an unlimited expansion of consciousness. If you can go to the depths of death as an option, then you do not limit any other option from entering the picture just short of actual death.

These brave souls had to know what others would do to try to stop them from meeting their goal, but they did not hold the thoughts of others in their mind, they only held their desire and ultimately understood, they held the power to do something about their situation despite what others may say or do. The truth, anyone who is captured, enslaved or held against their will, is always dealing with a battle of the mind. The captor is always attempting to overcome the individual's mind and will. If they can take the mind, then and only then will the captor actually have and maintain power. If the mind is not enslaved with the body, the mind will find a way out or draw freedom near and will never give the captor total satisfaction. The captor will always feel uneasy of an individual in their right mind, especially if that mind is able to gather and hold knowledge that further empowers the mind. It weakens the captor and shines light on the false construct of power.

Many surrender their power, because they devalue their own worth. It's an easy feat to succumb to. This could be done individually or collectively as a society.

The truth is you were worthy when breath was breathed into your body. You were worthy when you were set aside for a purpose before you were placed in your mother's womb. You are worthy, because nothing can separate you from the love or power of God. You are and will always be one with the Father in spirit and in truth. You are the reflection of God, the manifestation of the universe. All that it is, you are. You are worthy, because you have been manifested from the heavenly mind of God's creation into the earth. You are worthy, because you mattered enough to be created. You are worthy, because someone found you worthy enough to spend so much energy trying to pry away your worthiness and power. No one wastes time on anything or anyone they do not think holds value.

Consciously, before you took on a life and forgot your greatness, you knew you held the power within yourself. That is why this life you chose to experience did not appear to be such a daunting thing to take on. You knew that who you were could be born into a life that is categorically less desirable than most humans would petition and yet, you knew you could create a life beyond its limitations. You knew that your physical existence would not define your presence of power, but that your presence of power could dictate to creation. You knew that only what you believed would be. It's time to reset your mind back to its original factory setting – greatness is who I am, therefore I am a worthy being full of power and grace.

PART IV - FEAR

Fear Is Feedback

The greatest obstacle to creation of our heart's desire is fear. Fear of failure, fear of greatness, fear of wasted time and energy, fear of what we know and fear of what we do not know. Despite this fact, we have been created to indulge in the abundance of all that life has. We are equipped to experience and bring about joy, love, fun, patience, kindness and excitement. Though we are also equipped to deal with sadness, disappointment, rejection, projection, and the like, it is not intended to be who we are, nor are we to allow these emotions to linger, but to pass. Why? Because energy feeds and grows. Any energy that cannot bring about the desired state and grow into something great to attract more of its nature should only be utilized for transitioning and not built upon.

It would be a lie to say you can experience only good, joy and happiness. That is impossible. What you can do is control the impact life has on you and keep things in perspective. Remain aware that it is all feedback.

Since there is no limit to the possibility in which we can and will experience life, we must understand and name it all good. Yes, it is all good. Embrace it. Accept that it will all work out for our good, because it is all feedback. It is all direction and growth.

Despite this reality, we still hold a fear of life experiences and the emotional roller coaster that often accompanies. Nevertheless, it is not the scary, sad and ugly we fear as much as the wealth, success and progression. Why? Because if we have these things and experiences, we have something to lose. We are afraid of losing and failing. Especially if it is possible that others will know. We do not want to have what we desire and end up in a state in which we lack that which we desire and others see us in this vulnerable and contradictory state of being. This fear has us often waddling in constant fear and wonder if one move will end our high or progression. Is this the thing that will end it all? Can I

Law of First Thought

handle this change? Will this or that happen to me...? We fear the questions. We fear the answers. We fear the feeling of being helpless against it all.

Truth is fear has no real power. It is only an energy that holds questions and illusions of possibilities that may or may not ever happen. If you allow it to engulf you and your mind, it will then have a power it never had before in the fertile soil of your thoughts. When fear connects with your thoughts, it becomes empowered to create, dictate and direct your power of creation and the creative relationship you have with God.

Your thoughts are the most powerful source of creation you have. Anything that attaches to this source exploits the power it is attached to for its own gain, because in and of itself, it is powerless. If fear is exposed for what it is, it dissipates—as all shadows do when light is cast upon it. If you allow fear to act as a driving force, then it will take on the nature of power and control. You must always remain in control of your thoughts and regulate any fear that rears its head. You must accept, deal with, and disband fear with truth and self-light. There is no energy, no emotion--no feeling that has power over us, except the power we give it with our thoughts and attention.

The energy of fear is not bad in and of itself. It is not something to fight. It is just energy. This energy force is a sign, a warning and message giving us feedback about ourselves, others, and circumstances. It is leading, directing, questioning, and answering. We hold the power of action and the power to refrain from action in the face of fear. Never ignore energy, including fear. Be mindful so as not to fall victim to it. Always ask the question of the questioning energy to find out why it is here and what you must do next. It is important to discover why fear is even present and not fight it. Whatever you fight, you ignite. Whatever you are igniting, you are becoming one with it. You ever see people fight? Their arms and hands become entwined and they become one energy, one ball of flesh rolling around struggling for dominance.

Part IV – Fear

Fear is not in the air, unless it is vibrating from someone. Love is not in the air, unless it is overflowing out of someone. We hold the power and give it to the world through feelings and emotions. Our power is used to kill or give life, destroy or build up. You choose how your power will affect your world every day and every second of your life. Therefore, ask the question of fear in order to receive the feedback that will empower you to cancel fear's employment and hinder it's take over.

Love does not give birth to fear. However, if love and fear are present, many times the fear is what holds your attention, because you feel no harm from love. Fear, destruction, and the like hold your attention, because it holds possibilities of the unknown like no other energy. You watch and focus on it, waiting to see what it will do and what it will bring. All the time losing the love, the peace, and the joy that is around you when you are held captive by the darkness of fear. Like an armed robber, it talks you into giving it things. Until you break your gaze and realize it is just an illusion with a lot of questions of impossibilities, it will keep robbing you. Joy, peace, prosperity, and wealth will be fleeting because you keep allowing your power, your words, attention and thoughts to be used by fear. Talking about it, thinking about it, and making plans around it all steal from you. Take your power back, and you will take your life back.

Fear in the Shadows

Fear brings about questions that are sometimes necessary for our protection. It can be a beneficial tool to open our eyes. However, if we cannot control fear, we cannot afford to allow it within our space of creation. Why? Because fear is a halter and truly produces after its own nature. Fear begets fear. Fearful thoughts create fearful acts, and fearful manifestations that can only recreate the cycle over and over again. Until we are able to act in spite of our fear, this cycle will continue. We will have to do something different, like take courage and become aware.

Fear does not like to be questioned or examined, because it knows that if questioned effectively and evaluated, it will have to dematerialize. Fear understands that cognizance of its true nature will deem it not to be real. A shadow of reality searching for power to manifest through. Fear's only way to survive is through the power it takes from you.

If you allow fear to be anything other than a tool to bring about awareness, once it has any power, it will become your enemy. That is the only way it can stay in power. It must keep you captured to stay in control with relevance. The more captured and dependent you become of fear, the more empowered and necessary it becomes. Fear does not actually have a negative intent; it is only doing its job trying to protect us from doing and being something different than we already are. It likes homeostasis. It does not like change. It knows how to operate in our current state of being. It knows its place and power potential.

We do not like change in general. So fear is usually trying to help us stay right where we are for comfortability. Truth is all intentions are good intentions in the eye of the beholder of the intention. Though energies, like fear, may not have negative intention, when it is given power, it has a negative consequence. It was not created to be in power. It was only created as a warning and questioning mechanism. When it is allowed power and control it has not been created or conditioned to use effectively, it causes havoc. Fear is not an energy begotten of love or truth. It is a mechanism that should point you back into the direction of love and truth to answer the question it poses.

It is a shadow. A shadow allowed to linger as a consequence of the knowledge of good and evil. Fear is an aftereffect of knowing all possibilities that do or could plague our decision-making. It forms when you don't know what to do or think. A response to our inability to trust our own decisions. That is why we are instructed to shut the door behind us when we enter the secret place to pray, so the shadows are not welcomed. When you pray, you are commanding and conversing with your own spirit and the God within you. You must not allow shadows of doubt and fear to enter this powerful conversation and interaction because it has the ability to contaminate this sacred interchange.

Have you ever seen a shadow of yourself, hovering over the sidewalk and being walked over by passersby? When we allow the shadow's power and make them more real than they are, it is like seeing the feet of the passerby walk through our shadow and internalizing the footsteps passing over the shadow as if they are tangible and real impressions upon our body. Internalizing the illusion that somehow we are being destroyed by what we are seeing and falling victim to the illusion. This is self-deceit through the eyes of a shadow. Not being able to distinguish real from imagined is a product of living with shadows.

Falling victim to shadows cause us to foster a habit of building stories of victimization and apprehension that we tell ourselves over and over. Stories that destroy our sense of wholeness. Stories that bring death, instead of life to our own souls. We tell ourselves that love and possibility are not real for us and that the attacks, the words we tell ourselves are truer. Not realizing we made it true, we gave it power, we gave it feeling, we gave the stories value, and take away our own sense of wholeness and greatness. The shadow takes its unrighteous place on our throne, and we tell ourselves and then others, "I am broke. I am abused. I am neglected. I am in pain. I am crushed. I am unworthy, because someone else said or treated me as such." We gave away our power to define and recreate ourselves in our true image. We used our power of definition, the use of the "I am" statement to kill and limit ourselves. We took on a paradoxical nature. We allowed the shadow to tell us who we are and what we can or cannot be. Our power cannot only build, but can kill with just a thought, just a word, with our belief. That is why the shadows of fear cannot be allowed the ability to rule.

Self-Deception of the Second Nature

Many have heard the story about Adam and Eve and the tree of good and evil. I would like to give another perspective on this tree. If we can take a step back and realize that all Holy Scriptures of all religions are not talking about people, flesh or blood, but about consciousness. Every story, parable or proverb intends to awaken us to a deeper and more empowered mindset. They are to quicken our consciousness to who we are. If we understand the story of the tree from this perspective, we can then contextually become aware of our own tree of good and evil. The mindset of the tree of good and evil within us holds our first and second nature. The first nature of being like and in the likeness of God. The good and high consciousness. The second nature is defined, nurtured and born of the limitations of life and bodily experiences. The tree of life, of good and evil, reflects our duality of existence. We are both spirit and flesh. However, we can only operate in one nature at a time. Which one we will operate in and from is chosen each day, each second, each minute, each hour of each day.

Grappling with this duality is where the struggle for Adam and Eve arose. It is what we still struggle with often today. This story remains a personification of humanity's internal battle when faced with the many facets of itself. The responsibility, the sovereignty and the capacity is overwhelming and often confusing. The questions that mount confound the mind.

Adam and Eve illustrate the duality of our nature and how coming into the awareness of the other possibilities of ourselves captivates us. It also shows us how fear plays out when we attach to the second nature and forsake the first nature of who we are. The second nature often hypnotizes us to the point we forget the abundance and joy around us afforded by the first nature. From the fascination of the second nature we begin to recreate a new definition of who we are born of uncertainty. The second nature regulates by the shadows of conceivable iniquities within and around us. The first nature frees us. It allows us unlimited experiences and existences that do not take away, but uphold the strength of who we know ourselves to be in line with our higher consciousness. To the point that Adam and Eve were friends with the beast of the garden. They were in the midst of dangerous animals, by definition, but still knew and experienced peace that is beyond logical comprehension. A reflection of their higher consciousness

Taking part of the tree of knowledge means you become aware of the fact that you have more than one nature. That you have the ability to be like God and choose who you will be and what you will believe. This is a power that is amazing to have, and yet scary. It is scary because this ability is usually not matured to a level in which it is mastered for our advantage. That takes time and use. Without mastering our choice, we can become enthralled by the unlimited and unknown possibilities unfamiliar to us.

Though we like to deceive ourselves that we can save ourselves from this second nature, the truth is, it is who we are. We cannot be separate from what is a part of us. We are not usually conscious of the other aspects of who we are, so we believe they do not exist. Just because you are not aware of something, does not mean it does not exist. Adam and Eve did not come into a lesser consciousness when they partook of the tree, they became aware that there were other aspects of them they were not cognizant. Recognizing that I am that I am truly means that I am any and all things alerts us to our nature.

We must come to accept that God is not only good, he is also death, destruction, fire, rain, and births new worlds and experiences through painful means that are still, by definition, good because of the intention and use. God is not separate from death; death is a tool to birth life. One cannot exist without the other. God is all things. He has the capacity to be and do all things, and yet not be or define himself by any one thing. This is who you are. But like Adam and Eve, the weight is sometimes so heavy that you forget exactly who you are and hide in the comfort of your lower vibrations of the second nature.

We don't want to experience letdowns or disappointments. Our second nature attempts to keep us from doing anything that puts us in the wake of that possibility. We do not want to risk for the fear of failing, even though we have to go past risk to get to opportunities and move toward success. Second nature will not only have you fearful to move, but have you attempt to stop others from moving forward for fear they will reach goals you have yet to believe you can reach for yourself.

We confuse ourselves into thinking that if we expect the worst, when it comes, we won't be so caught off guard and can stifle the pain. This protection of self deems itself warranted by our subconscious mind stuck in second nature. Over time, it would appear that this mindset protects us more than the original first nature of love, honesty, openness, risk, and freedom. This first nature causes us to walk with dangerous beast and fear no evil. It empowers us to name and give nature to animals three and four times our size. It authorizes us to have dominion in our lives and against energies and ideals that appear stronger on the outside of us. This nature takes away the worry for what we would eat, drink, wear or sleep, because we realize that we can create or ask for it, and it will be so. This is who you are and who you were before the human experience brought in questions for you to contend with.

Learning how to balance the two natures effectively so not to fall victim to our lesser existence is imperative. Allow the lesser nature to raise questions. You will realize that it will only bring you back to the awareness of your higher first nature. Do not fight, struggle or try to separate yourself from your second nature. It serves a purpose, as all things do. However, it is not the place you should lead and drive your life. It is helping you to remember who you are and solidify the answers to the questions, so that you will know without a shadow of a doubt that you are in the Garden of Eden, you lack nothing. You are whole, worthy, complete and one with the Father, no matter what it may look like or what questions are posed to you. Therefore, there is nothing to be ashamed of and nothing to hide from. You are the power. You are the light. You are everything God is and therefore everything is possible in and for you.

Everlasting Fear

The possibility of being without creates a fear that is usually acted upon. It triggers our primal flight or fight impulse. You are a creator, so you will desire to create to fill a void, solve a problem, and heal what is broken. However, this reaction is often tainted by fear. Therefore, when you create in reaction to fear, you can only manifest a harvest or outcome that looks like the seed sown.

Two spirits can trigger the creative process. One is creation and the other is reaction. Notice that these words have the same letters, but the c in creation is first and the c in reaction is in the middle of the act. If you are in creation, you see first; but if you are in fear, you can't see anything until you are in the midst of it.

Often our creations are reactions of the past. When we have created in response to the past, we live in everlasting fear induced realities. We must be mindful of the past and why we did and do the things we do. Without resolving the past, we allow it to maintain a hold on our future.

We often think we can walk away from things without replicating and projecting its energy in some form or fashion. If our home, career, or bank accounts look different today than yesterday, we think yesterday has been left in the past. Not so. There is no space in time. There is only now. This moment also encompasses yesterday, today, and tomorrow. Today was orchestrated yesterday, illustrated now, and creating tomorrow. There is no separation in time or energy. It is and will always be now. That is why it is important to take control of your ability to create, so that you can create, recreate, end, and start anew whenever you desire.

Adam and Eve, Christ, Buddha, Muhammad, Mami Wata, Gandhi, the guy who built your neighborhood, the guy that set off bombs or local fires, great grandchildren, new countries and new worlds of the future were with us yesterday, are all with us now and impact tomorrow. We are either impacted or being impacting. That is why re-visioning history without dealing with the truth of it allows us to repeat it and fall victim to the lies we tell ourselves.

The same energy, the same place of powerlessness that is within you remains with you until change occurs. It is not what is outside of you that must change, but it is your mindset, your self-worth, and your self-knowledge that brings the change. If they do not change, we walk in the patterns of yesterday today and set a trap for tomorrow.

For example, we get out of an abusive house, get our own family and life, and we abuse coworkers, emotionally abandon our spouses, and drive our kids to a level of success to the point that we neglect to nurture their soul. It's the same spirit replicating itself in a different time and place through other avenues. We lie to ourselves and say we have overcome the past and are different from our parents; however, the fear of repeating the pattern actually causes us to be more creative in our powerlessness and reproduce in their likeness in other ways.

Whatever has your attention has your life. Fear has no power, but if you give it your attention it will take over your life and become one of the most powerful enemies within you that you could muster. Fear usually creeps in through doubt and past experiences that have not been dealt with. What happened in the past usually fosters a wheel of thoughts that play routinely in the mind and ultimately in the family, society or cultural structures that help maintain the effects and hinder the healing.

This is why it is important to be honest with ourselves and do the work to heal ourselves. If we do not do the work, we live with lies and pain that is then passed on to our children. It is exercised in our marriages, workplaces, academic standing and the like. This is where the sins of the father or mother are passed and manifested upon the children (Exodus 34:7). The children will cry out, act out, and bleed out the sins and iniquities of their parents, their societal woes religious and cultural suppressions. We are more than our brother's keeper, we are our brother, and our brother is who we are. We all carry the burdens and scars of fears and lies that were not dealt with before us, but bandaged and passed on for with which someone else has to deal. Just as we hold our ancestor's strengths, we hold their weaknesses. Many of us don't even realize from where our strengths and weaknesses come. We only know the wounds we bear. Constantly searching for the answers that cannot be found by searching our lifetime alone. Dealing with questions that were never our question to answer. Burdens that were never our burden to bear.

Being awakened to this empowers us. The reason we are empowered is because duality exist in all things. If the burden is present, the power to overcome it is as well. There is no good without evil, no up without down, no right without left, no known without unknown. If the burden is there, the power to relieve the burden is as well. We must now turn our attention away from what has held us captive to find the answer to free our souls and minds. It is waiting on us.

How do we know it is present? Because nothing is created without its equal and opposite counterpart. We have the awareness in this moment and the power right now that can destroy the pitfalls of yesterday. The power to create the path we desire making it straight. We can kill the fear that haunts us and the shadow that haunted those before us.

Fear of Change

Are you bubbling up with questions? What will I choose? Who will I be? What is the new name I give myself? What will I do next? What thought or belief will I utilize or transform? Will fear keep me right where I am? Questions I am sure rise to the surface for answers. Not having answers to these questions many times creates anxiety. Having the answer and knowing what one must do to bring about change can also cause anxiety. It is not just work you realize you must do to change, but one must also face all the unknowns that come with change.

The reason we often do not make the changes we need is because humans in general fear change. Not because change in and of itself is scary—though it can be—but the truth of the matter is that we fear not having the right answers. We fear the change not being what we hoped it would be. We fear that we will not know how to operate and maintain a new level of thinking or living if the change and risk taking pays off. We fear being right back where we started after tasting a better life or experience. We fear disappointment. We fear making mistakes. We fear living without fear and we fear living with it.

The possibility of failure or returning back to a state of undesirability keeps us from making the change. Who will I be? What will they expect of me? Will I let them down? Will I let myself down? Will they still only see me as who I was? Can I be anything other than what I know right now? How do I know what I truly want if I never experienced it? All are questions laced with fear. The fear of the unknown. Fear from knowledge of good and evil. Instead of focusing on the fact you may experience all the good the tree has, you are captivated on the possibility of experiencing all the evil the tree possesses. It has you hiding, searching and reasoning your way out of reaching for the good.

Not knowing is such a vulnerable and scary place if you allow it to be. Have you ever just stopped to consider what it feels like when you say, "I don't know?" Or have you felt that pit in your stomach that comes from not knowing? When someone asks you a question in the midst of you trying to find an answer to a question you are muddling your way through, have you ever realized that you lash out at that person who is asking you another question? You already feel like you don't have the answer to one question, now here comes another. It's like your mind is on lock and you can't think. You can't connect. You are lost. It's because we think we have to know and when we don't, we feel exposed. We don't have to have all the answers. We have to be okay with the knowledge we do have.

Many times you will not have all the answers until you can trust yourself enough to walk out the first step toward the goal. As you walk the path, more will be revealed unto you. Part of the journey is discovery. Not always knowing anything other than who you are and what you desire. The feeling that one must always know is created from one's childhood in which shame is placed on a person for not knowing. This product of shame is a sibling of fear. Shame usually brings the question - what does it say about you if you don't know? Your new answer will be – "it means nothing, because I am always in the process of discovery. When I need to know, I will be still long enough to receive the answer clearly from the peace within me. I am the answer, I am."

If you ever read the story of Adam and Eve, the stories of Elisha, the story of Jacob wrestling with the angel, and the story of so many in the Holy Scriptures of any religion, you see this fear of not knowing manifesting itself from an internal battle to an outward struggle. Struggling with the unknown. Not having the answer makes us feel less than worthy of what we desire. We desire to be as all-knowing as God. We desire, above all things, to be powerful, to be aware, and to know. We desire to live beyond the limits of our humanity and in the infinite of our spirit. When it appears we are not taping into the spirit possibility causes us to question the infinite within us and lean on the humanity for answers to fill the gap.

If we don't have the answer to our purpose, we feel invisible. If we don't know our goals, we feel aimless. If we don't have a title, we have no identity. All these validations and standards of being we create so that we can know ourselves and define ourselves in a tangible manner. Without them, we don't think we exist. The sad thing is, these answers, these ways of validation are external. They are, on the surface, limited definitions. Many times the titles make us sound more important and stable than we actually feel.

We are always creating and discovering the answer in the right time and at the right moment. If we let go of all the other stuff, we would make space and stillness for the answer to reveal itself from within us. Then, the outside title would be less necessary. If we remove our definitions and expectations of what it or we should look like, we would see that the answer was always and is always there waiting for us to be known. Knowing self first, allows all the other paths to be revealed in relationship to who I AM.

The last reason we fear that we must change, is that we fear that who we are meant to be will not be enough. Who we are may not live up to the idea we hoped for ourselves or others hoped for us. We fear we are average, not special by outward definition. However, outward definitions should never be allowed to paint your abundance into a box acceptable to anyone or anything other than your own soul's satisfaction. When you connect with the authenticity of yourself, all fear will dissipate and every avenue created intentionally for you in all your unique glory will be made available and revealed unto you.

Be okay knowing that we are powerful, and yet, we are not. That we are enough, and yet, we are not. That we are gods, and yet, we are not. We are the paradoxical duality that exists, and we don't often know which side of ourselves we are on. My friend, when you boil it all down, where your fear lie is in this truth – the truth that you have yet to discover and know thyself. You have not known or accepted all aspects of you. Can I free you today and tell you that you don't have to have or know all the answers? You just have to be bold enough and have enough faith to know that whatever and whoever you are right now is enough today. From this place of acceptance of you being more than enough, the answers and direction will freely surface. You are good right where you are, as you are.

PART V - EXPERIENCE IS A LIAR AND YET HOLDS ALL TRUTH

Experience Speaks

You knew everything until you forgot. Now do this in remembrance of you.

In the beginning before you were placed in your mother's womb, you knew who you were and the power you held. You knew that you and the Father were one. You knew that with the Father was the word, and that word formed you. You knew that you were the creator's thought formed and manifested by a word. You understood that whatever you thought came to pass instantly because it was connected with the power of creation that has created all things including you. You knew that you were in the likeness of your creator and, therefore, could act accordingly in similar nature.

As you thought, your thought formed and materialized into being in your experience. Your thought was the word as your creator's thought was His word. When you were placed in the womb, you heard a word from a breath of life. From that word seeded inside of your spirit a new thought of you was established. From this thought accepted, you thought yourself into flesh, and instantly, you were.

In the womb you sent forth energy messages of thought to your host carrier – your mother. You thought that you were hungry. This thought sent the energy of hunger to the mother. Then your thought, which is also your word, manifested causing the mother to feed you through her. Your mother's body, acting in its law and nature, responded to the word and the thought you had. Whatever you thought, it was so. You thought thirst. You needed more energy, more space, more

Law of First Thought

fluid, or whatever was necessary in the womb, and it was so. The body responded, the mind receptive to you responded.

The energy from your word would cause her body to give up its own nutrients and its own life so you could live, because you, the child, knew who you were. You operated from a greater power of knowing than even your mother. You operated fully in your spiritual mind of self. Your mother succumbed to the thoughts, the words, and the energy that was inside of her. She responded to the word and feeling. Her body instinctively knew the law and operated in accordance. She was in agreement and together you operated as one.

Once the child is born, this oneness begins to shift, but not enough to forsake the child's sense of self. Initially, the child cries out. If you pay attention, each cry is distinct. It never cries without intention. Though the language of the baby is not understood verbally, it is still emotionally felt. As a mother or caretaker, even in this infantile stage, there is still a response to the inarticulate thoughts of the child reverberated with sounds, even when one is sleeping. The mother wakes up because they know the child needs to be changed. They sense the child is uncomfortable. They hear the hunger cry, the thirsty cry, the cry of uncertainty, and the need for comfort cry. Each time, responding to the word. Even a mother who has lost her child in the womb or early in its life from Sudden Infant Death Syndrome (SIDS, or some other unexpected situation, she can sense when the life has left the body because something has changed—a disconnection has occurred. Before seeing with the eye or hearing with the ear, the spirit knows no matter how it wants to deny reality. It knew the oneness connection in which it answered to had severed.

The entire time the child is growing, it still thinks and believes that it is one with God, that the word in its mouth has power, and that its thought brings all it desires. In the very early stages, the child never doubts who it is. It does not doubt that those around it will not take care of him or her. It believes its cries will be answered.

As the child grows and individuality becomes the focus, doubt walks in, as well as confusion, neglect, fear and the like. The child is told to self-sooth and rely on itself. They are yelled at, ignored, cast down, punished, and the love appears to have become conditional. They are seen as needy and dependent and what was beautiful and special, now becomes burdensome and too much. The child is labeled bad, grumpy, and other negative labels. The words and feelings toward the child begin to feel like cruel energy from the mouth of the ones they thought would love them unconditionally. The individuals they saw as their god manifestation on earth, now desire them to prove themselves worthy of their time and attention. The cries go unanswered or are met with joyless faces, anger, disappointment or strangers paid to care, but not to love them. The child begins to question its own thoughts and beliefs of its worthiness and lovability. The questions in excess overload the mind.

The serpentine situations of life bring more questions for the child. The questions that the child believed it once knew the answer to, he now doubts that answer. He now questions himself and allows doubt, confusion and exposure to come into his experience. This in and of itself is not bad.

Questions are important. They bring awareness, direction, revelation and so much more. However, when you are not equipped to deal with the questions and have no answer of substance as a child's mind has yet to devise. The child grasps for anything to feel safe, comfortable and smart. They lash out, lash inward and try to figure out some way to comfort, protect or cover themselves in the moment.

The child no longer knows who they are, so they move to discover itself in other ways. The older the child gets and the more people, places and institutions come in to validate, dictate, devalue or label the child, the more the original thought that "I am god, all is well, and my thoughts of goodness toward the world will bring goodness toward me" wanes. Self-talk in the voice of the parents, teachers, counselors, and others grow as a heaviness chipping away as the child's sensibility. The veracity of change kills the child's hopes and dreams. The child is fearful of being disappointed and being a disappointment.

The more the child integrates into the greater society, the more the child begins to sees the possibility of its own limitation. Not because that is who they are, but because that is all that continues to be pointed out to them. They were fine with who they were, until they were told otherwise. They were cute, fun, and wonderful until they were no more. Conditions, limitations, expectations, definitions of good and bad quantifiers complicated things. Now the child tells another story about itself, its God, and those it held in trust.

Eating from the tree of good and evil opens the child's eyes to frustration, to hate, to pain, to loneliness, and the original thought of self is replaced with another thought— a second nature thought tainted with the idea that "You are bothersome, you are a disappointment, you are a burden, and you are not worthy of attention." Comparisons are made to neighbor's kids, church kids, schoolmates, athletes, science geeks, siblings, or the parents' own past and present accomplishments or failings. Marginalized because of accents, color of skin, and texture of hair or economic status of family. All of these new experiences, thoughts, and feelings overcome the original or first thought of self. A new thought, contrary to the original one, is established and sits on the throne of the child's mind. From this place of distortion and breakdown, the child creates its image of self and the life he is worthy of living based on the thoughts of another—a life less than dreamed, a life less than what God himself desired and co-created before the child was placed in the womb. Possibilities of limitations thrust upon him. Shadows cast upon his light of greatness.

The child creates out of a broken and conditional place, unlike its true original nature. The child rebels and becomes angry, internalizing its pain. It does whatever it can to get back what it feels it has lost. It tries to figure out who it is and its purpose of being. It keeps on doing and working, trying to get back to that good place. If it could only earn it, be worthy of it, be good enough for a glimpse of the feeling of whole, good or unconditional love. Maybe if it wins this, gets that degree, married that person, attends this church, earns this title, lives in that neighborhood or drives this car will it finally be who and what they always wanted to be.

Law of First Thought

Unless reassured that the changes are beneficial and not personal. Reassured that they are still loved, that their word still creates, they are good, and their thoughts will be answered in fullness, then the other thoughts of lack, hurt, and pain take over. The remaining parts of the life journey can be plagued with the torturous attempt to reclaim its tattered soul's wholeness. For many this effort can often be too much with which to deal. Healing seems like such a challenge. Instead of healing, many create coping mechanisms that protect them allowing the wounds and questions to fester under the guise of normalcy.

If we look back through our life, even if our total trek was not so dire, we can find the points in life where the shifting from our original nature and thoughts of ourselves changed. We can begin to see how the experiences of life began to shape and tell our stories. They redefined who we were. Maybe the experiences occurred later in life. No matter when the experience happened, the change of mind still occurred. The questions came with the same inability to answer, so the experience gave you an answer that cast a shadow on your worthiness. The experience was louder than the truth within you.

Were you validated? Were you affirmed? Were you allowed to believe that you and the Father are one despite life's happenings? Did you realize that you were always operating in oneness even when you were not aware of it or made to feel worthy of it? Were you made to believe that you are a sinner, a wretch who will hopefully one-day gain forgiveness or mercy to be loved enough? Do you know that you do not have to qualify to be who you are? You only need to choose and accept who you are.

Did you experience that life was a gift, or was it a struggle? Could you depend on the ones you loved or those who said they loved you, or did you fend for yourself? Did other things or people seem more important than you? Did you have to sacrifice your good for the overall good of the family or someone's career? Was your parent a pastor, a doctor, a missionary, an alcoholic, or unknown? Did you have to sacrifice for others you did not know or care about? Were you told that your sacrifice was good and yet you do not know how to rectify that sense of good with the loss you still felt? Did your mother or father sacrifice your happiness for the love of a new spouse or significant other, which, in turn, sacrificed your happiness, stability, or peace? Does and did any of these experiences define you? Do they still define you?

So many experiences occur in our lives that leave residue on the walls of our minds and in the corners of our self-worth. We take something away from every experience. If we are not aware, we can take away a reality that is absent of the true reflection of who we are and can be. Experience is a good teacher, but it is also a great liar, beware. Remember that if you feel that you have lost anything, there is also a storage waiting on you to choose from that was created in opposition to the loss. You cannot have one experience or anything without the opposite being created and present as well. If you felt unworthy, worthiness has been given to you. If you lost something, then something else was created for you to find. If you were hungry, moments in which there is no lack or hunger have been created for you. You only need to become aware of that reality and turn your attention away from the lie of the lower consciousness. Arise.

Awake. There is nothing you do not and cannot have; it is all waiting on you.

I Create from Experience

Experience and thought are complementary. You are always experiencing your thoughts and your thoughts are always producing experiences. These thoughts command and rule the direction of our lives and choices. Many times the experiences give us feedback that is not actually sound, true or beneficial. It is just feedback of the moment. However, when we have experiences, there are emotions that are attached that mesmerize us. When you have emotions and physical activity occurring at once, it overloads the mind's logic and allows messages to be sent directly to the subconscious mind that are deposited as current fact. If you are not conscious or on guard to the thoughts filtering in, you can and will allow these thoughts and ideas to set up shop as a new law to live by instead of it being categorized as momentary information.

When this occurs, the only way to remove the laws established are through another experience. The new experience for change can be physical, spiritual, mental or emotional. Whatever way it is experienced, it must impress well enough to initiate change.

For example, if a child is told not to touch something because it is hot, the child almost instinctively gravitates to the exact thing from which we are telling them to stay away. The thought of the experience of hot to the child is not resolved enough to want to refrain from acting. They desire to know through experience how to define and understand hot. They want to know if what you say is true or can they come to know that their idea of hot is more real than the notion you are narrating.

Their curiosity to know holds their attention. It is not until they finally experience getting burned on a stove that they respect it enough to be cautious around it. The pain, the heat, the scarring, and the unpredictability all send messages into the subconscious mind that breed significance. Before the experience of hot, the child's belief of hot was limiting. It was not as real as the experience became at the moment of being burned.

The second experience was more impactful and overrode the initial experience and belief of hot. From this intense experience the child generates a new law about hot, fire, stove and anything else relating to hot. They also come to respect other's ideas given to them, like their parent(s), because they found the parent's warning to be trustworthy. The child further believes that hot is serious, dangerous, scary, painful, and can cause ugly irreversible damage. Even if the child does not experience the irreversible damage, they accept it as possible because one part of the warning from the parent has been deemed sound. Therefore, the child accepts all other possibilities that come with hot

As they grow older, they may become a chemist, astronomer, or chef--where fire and stoves may have different meanings and possibilities for them. As they experience fire and heat in a way that is creative, transitional, workable, controllable, and important, then their thought of fire, heat, and the stove change as well. The experience in the present changes the experience of the past. It puts things in context and removes the generalities of the past. This new experience changes the thoughts of the person, which, in turn, changes the belief and the relating words spoken from the belief system of the person on the idea of fire, heat, and stoves in relationship to danger and destruction. Because they have the skills, tools, and means of dealing with and overcoming fire; respect and balance replaces the fear. The new thought empowers them in their work and efforts and takes away the idea of helplessness. The unknowns are known, the distortions are rectified, and their own power is revealed. A new experience created a new thought.

Experience Is Not Always A Great Teacher

Experiences are only possibilities. They should never be our guide of measure and infinite truth, because all you have to do is experience something else to disprove or overcome the prior experience in order for it to be deposed. Therefore, never make an experience your ruler, just a teacher of that moment that may or may not have been absolute in its resolve in teaching. It is just like your elementary, junior high, high school teachers, and college professors. They all played their parts; some were better than others. They all taught different things and had different styles of teaching. You learned things about yourself from each of them. You may have taken inferences that were of their own bias and not really about you. However, the labels of good, bad, smart, dumb, mediocre, lazy, driven, etc., were placed upon you by the experience of that year, that month, or that exam.

I had great teachers and not so great teachers. Some told me that my race and gender limited my possibilities in life, and others told me that I could fly to the moon and back. Some told me I was a leader, and others told me that I needed to get in my place and stay in it. I talked too much or I did not talk enough. All the labels and experiences were giving feedback about me, my abilities, and possibilities based on moments in time from another's perspective. The truth is relative in these situations. Many times these opinions were nothing more than indictments based on the teacher's own unresolved understandings and limitations of themselves, or others like me, projected upon me. All had the intention of molding my inside according to what they thought was best according to their ideals. It was rarely about praising my individual light. It was rarely about calling to my spirit or desire. Many of them led by the dictation of the system they were employed were doing what they were hired to do. Shape me and the writings on the wall of my mind to have thoughts and aspirations acceptable to the greater system they abided by. Others, few and unique angels as they were, told me to rest in my freedom and to dream beyond all possibilities.

So many voices. Every day and every year I have received a constant contradiction and fluctuation of self-esteem, self-worth, and wonderings as I evolved. Holding on to the words that gave me comfort and fighting those that did not. Teachers—either actual teachers or experiences that teach—must be put in the proper connotations, so they will not be our god and our guide in self-education, awareness, and creation. Experience, is not always a great teacher. It is feedback and awareness of the moment. It is an assistant with questions and mirrors.

Like all teachers, experiences come with its biases and distortions. They have agendas that may be beneficial, and others are not. In the end, we must make the choice of what we will believe about ourselves and our possibilities, allowing the limitations of others and the unlimited possibilities from others be accepted or denied in our own belief system. Just because a system is in charge of your mind and future, does not mean it knows the truth of you. Nor does it know who you were created to be. That truth and possibility only lives within you.

PART VI – THE WORK

Part VII – Responsibility

Question the Thought

We often hold on to old thoughts out of loyalty to those who taught them to us or to those who we hold in high regard, because they still believe in them. We do not want to show disloyalty, or worse, we do not want those we love or believe in to be wrong. These individuals are usually our parents, teachers, grandparents, religious leaders, society, culture, race, ethnicity, government, etc. Questioning appears to be one of the hardest things with which I've seen human beings deal. They don't like to be questioned and they don't want to ask questions, because they don't want answers that will cause them to have to change. Lord, have mercy, if change is required. We would rather deal with the dysfunction we know rather than change to receive the peace we don't know. We would rather manipulate disorder to make it look like order, instead of doing the hard work of confronting and changing. The truth is that we all know what needs to be done, but it is something about the question and having to deal with the answer that is a stomach turner.

No matter how hard it may appear to be, we must do the work and question everything and everyone. We must ask why is this being said or done. What is the impact on me and those around me? Why has there been no change? What is the change that needs to occur? What will it look like if I do not make a change in thought or behavior? What will it look like if I do make a change in thought and behavior? The question holds power and direction. It gives answers you cannot receive or create without the question first being posed. We must dispel the myth that questioning is disrespectful and unnecessary. It is a tool we have mistakenly used against ourselves and others instead of in behalf of. Don't fear the question. Do not be as Adam and Eve and get so overwhelmed you forget who you are and where you are. Just seek the best and highest possible answer, not the perfect or expedient answer.

When you have the answer, question it until you are sure enough to move forward with confidence and no regret, no matter what. The question helps to make the vision clear. Once you have a clear vision you can further write or rewrite your path with clarity and intention.

Forgive

Forgiveness is a big part of effective creation. What you do unto another, you do unto yourself. If you hold things against others, then these things, according to law, should and will also be held against you. The negativity you desire for another shall also be desired for you. Because you desire them and create the law of unworthiness, hate, and limitation, then when you are creating, these laws will be in place for you as well. You are a creator and your laws are true in absolution for your belief system. So be mindful of your thoughts and your contempt. It is best to operate in love and forgiveness so that the law and energy you send out will come back to you in a form you so desire for you.

Forgiveness is not for others; it is for you. Forgiveness allows freedom of soul. It allows freedom in your creation and removes any possible limitation. That does not mean you let things go and allow others to do what they want to you. You still have a responsibility to hold value and stand guard over the vessel of the greatness that you are.

One of the greatest gifts you can give yourself is forgiveness. Freedom of unlimited, unconditional love of self to create on your worthy behalf. You forgive because you deserve forgiveness. You forgive to be free. You need to be free in all that you create, so that your creation is not limited or hindered by other thoughts. You forgive to grant freedom to others to do the same. You receive what you have first given and give what you too desire of and for yourself. Whenever you give or sow, you are first giving and sowing unto yourself. Everything is about you inclusively, though not specifically. When you forgive you release others from your mind's space to focus on creating for you. Forgiveness frees you to love and provide for you.

When you ask God or the universe to forgive you, you are asking for the old thoughts and commands to be released and a clean slate for a new creation to be formed. You are asking to be released from the bounds of yesterday's thoughts and actions. This is necessary, because as humans, our emotions and life can get the best of us and we will contemplate and toil with things endlessly that we do not realize are sticking to our spirits and clinging on the walls of our imaginations. Remember that the angels, the universe, and the creation process must obey the orders that come from you. If you keep thoughts around in your mind, they will help those connected to the thoughts to continue to stick around physically because you are keeping them around mentally.

You may get signals of discomfort letting you know that this may not be the greatest thing to do or say, but no bullhorn is going to go off and say this is not a good thought. It is up to you to listen to the still small voice. The universe holds no judgment. It only obeys the commands from the throne of your mind. So why not free it to operate unrestricted through the loving and merciful move of forgiveness.

Do You First Love Yourself

After you forgive yourself make sure you love yourself with your whole heart. Not selfishly, but self-fully. Fully fill yourself with love in, through and around you. Abandon any thought, person, place or thing that prevents or steals this possibility. Love is the greatest and most powerful tool for healing, creation, transformation and intentional aligned manifestation you have. You are love because you were created from, through and by love. Love is your first, only and real nature. Love operates and is present in all things. Love can take any form and show up in any experience. Love is powerful enough to be strong and weak. It can be right and wrong. It can be all things, and yet is not definable. Love is good. It is God. It is you. If you give love, you are giving yourself. If you receive love, you are receiving yourself back to you. Problem is we are quick to disown, reject and relinquish love every time it takes a form we cannot identify with or wish. When we block it from outside, we block it inside as well. Remember you are always doing unto you first.

So, do you love yourself? Do you love yourself first? This law of self-love has set other laws in motion. We often confuse this law. We think we are to love another before we love ourselves. This is not true. When the idea that we were first loved by another or in the idea the Christ or Buddha or Muhammad loved the people more than they loved themselves, or that God loved his creation first before self, this is not true. All forms of greatness and love do not love anything or anyone outside of itself first--they first loved themselves. From this place of authentic self-love and wholeness, they gave who they were. They loved you enough to love themselves first, search, receive and manifest who they were. Who they were, was of benefit for others, but if they did not love themselves enough to manifest within themselves who and what they were, they could not have poured out from a self-full place. They showed us how to love our authentic selves so that we could embrace who we were first. After you know and love yourself, then you can rise to the level of greatness established for you out of love. You cannot be contradictory to love and receive what is given only to and through love. Hate does not receive love. Because love is always present, even in darkness, the light of love calls out in the darkness of hate to the love that exists in the shadow. When open to receive, love can choose to answer. When love answers, hate takes a seat because two opposing energies cannot exist at one time. If one chooses to keep hate over love, then love is not received. It only stands at the door waiting to be chosen and received.

Love is not always about outward expressions. Love is a real state of being. It is energy, not an action. You can say that you did nothing but good to others and that you are a good person that loves yourself, but evaluate your life and relationships to see if this is truth. There are laws you have established that have allowed you to be in relationships that are not balanced, that are abusive, that are not validating, that are absent of respect and honor, that are not life-giving, and that have you playing second fiddle or sometimes fifth. This is a sign that a lack of love or worthiness may be present in you. We often confuse the sacrifice with love, but it is the purpose of the sacrifice that is love. If there is no goal, but to prove sacrifice, that is not love. That is sacrifice. Love has an objective of greater and higher aim than merely sacrifice.

You may be saying the right words. It may appear that you love yourself by what you wear and how you carry yourself on the outside with others. You know the conversation you are having with yourself in the dark and when you are alone. You know the rotten, soiled thoughts of self you have. Either created by you or given to you by a parent, ex-lover, friend, religious leader, or some other person of authority or experience. These thoughts of worthiness are usually developed in childhood and exacerbated in later stages of your life in relationship with others. Take the time to do the evaluation and find yourself in the dark.

When you realize the truth, accept it and work from there. What is your first thought, how did it become a foundational thought, and what other thoughts have grown from and live from the branches of this thought? Who are you now? How do you desire to love yourself? Are you looking for others to validate you because you do not? Are you looking for others to give you life? Are you sacrificing your love in unworthy and lifeless people, places, things, and deeds? Do you revel in the words and accolades of others? When you see your house, car, clothes, hair, or life, do you say to yourself "They will be so jealous, they will be so happy, they will be so mad?" They, they, they. If there is a they and not an I in your conversations with self or others, there is a thought distortion in your foundation, which finds wholeness in the lives, mouths, accolades, and definitions of others.

You are looking for love and validation outside of self, therefore you don't first love you. You are waiting for someone or something else to give you love and find you worthy of love. You are waiting for someone or something to give you what only you can give yourself. However, if you don't first give love to yourself, you will only receive whatever the replacement of love is that you are feeding off in the obscurities of your mind.

God first gave to himself and created from the fullness of Him. Jesus first gave, healed and took the time to awaken to himself and gave from this fullness. Buddha, Muhammad and many other teachers, prophets, guru's and others first gave and sought themselves for themselves and gave from within the fullness and awareness of that which is within them. That is why they are so great and their names will always be known. They searched to know, think and be like God, met themselves and shared with the world their awakened selves.

I Am Whole

Be grateful and multiply, then realize that is who you are.

It is essential that you, as a creator, see yourself as whole and complete in every way. When you see yourself as lacking, then lack will present itself in your experience in some form or fashion. You lack nothing. There is nothing you do not have and cannot create and manifest.

Learn to be grateful in the wholeness of who you are so that the energy of completeness can resonate in your life. Thank God for always seeing you as the wholeness and complete creation He created. This view He has of you is valuable. It is a gift given to you entrusted for you to echo back to Him and the world. It is vital to your life because it is the true nature of you. Thank God for opening your eyes to the truth He sees in you. Receive the truth of this blessing that you are whole and you lack nothing. Life has not taken anything away from you; it increases and expands you through great awareness and awakening every day. The questions continue to point you back to the truth of who you are so that you can choose your true nature and not the lies the experience may present.

You and the Father are one. All that the Father has and is, you are. From this day forward, strive to abide in that truth where you and He dwell as one. Not for any reason other than resting in the nature that holds your greatest power and confirmation of your soul. Be thankful for your beauty, perfection, love, and the eyes to see it. Accept your original thought that you are whole, beautiful, and perfectly imperfect. You are love, peace, joy, abundance, and truth. See, validate, and rest in this place this is the only true thought – I am whole and lack nothing. This is love of self that will last forever and will give birth to all your heart's desires.

Be grateful minute by minute in everything and everywhere. Gratitude and love raises your energy high to a vibration in which you touch and see the face of God and through the eyes of God.

Your Prayer Is Your Wish, So Wish Wisely

Too often, we think that prayer is some sweet and humble begging session in which special words are used to get us what we want or a sign that we are loved and validated. Other times, we use it as a to-do item and just check it off the list with no real awareness or connection with the prayer we say. It is an automatic response before bed, before a meal, or whenever we're in need. Prayer is more important than that. It is a tool for universal communication. It vibrates, commands, asks, answers, calls and creates. It is a tool for powerful creation in which you make yourself consciously aware

Law of First Thought

of your spirit and the unseen around you that is one with you. The universe is always waiting to communicate and work on your behalf. That is the lawful setup we fail to utilize.

Prayer is your communication with God, the universe, the angels, ancestors and all that is unseen. Though prayer respectively is a time of awareness to communicate with spirit, prayer is actually occurring every time you speak. The universe is not on hold when you are cursing people out, angry at your children or going through a divorce proceeding. When you speak, you say a prayer. You are in constant communication and the universe is in constant working mode bringing you experiences in line with your thoughts, energy and words. The universe is in full operation with and around us at all times. Every second of the day. You pray every time you think a thought and meditate on that thought. You are praying every time you move a thought into a feeling. You pray with every moan, and every tear. You pray with each praise and every joyous conversation. This is all prayer. That is why speaking should not be done indiscriminately but intentionally.

PART VII- RESPONSIBILITY

Choose Ye This Day

You cannot lie to yourself or change the mind of another, nor can another person change your mind for you, just as God cannot and will not override your gift of choice and dominion over your life. You are the only power over you. You are the only one that can choose to surrender your power, use your power or marry your power to something or someone else. The choosing is always yours. No one chooses for you. It is your gift of free will.

You are always in the process of choosing—choosing what you will believe and what you will not, what you will do and what you will not. You can allow others to influence that choice or not. You can choose to do what you have always done or not. Even if a parent or spouse chose for you at one time or another, you still had the power to align yourself with that choice or not. Over and over, again and again we choose. It is a choice to obey, conform, or not. You are still responsible and in control. You are even in control to choose not be in control, if you choose.

Judge Not, But In All Things, Be Wise as a Serpent

One of the primary keys of intentional creation we often miss after forgiveness, love, gratitude, accepting responsibly for ourselves and our thoughts is removing judgement. Judgement is hard because we are constantly looking to find and define what is good, bad, right, wrong, up, down, etc. However, in creation there is no room for judgement. All creation is good by definition. Creation is good, amazing, purposed and our overall desired nature. It is who we are. It is a reflection of our being. We are good. We must see ourselves good and therefore, our creations are good and good for us. When

Law of First Thought

you judge your creation, you are judging yourself. When you apply judgement, you apply limitation. When you judge, you are defining and naming a thing according to the judgement and out of alignment with the good intended.

Sure we get confused, caught up and distracted in life. Life happenings consume our thoughts and the after math that can sometimes come about in life's manifestations. Despite this, we must take heed that in the process of creation, no judgement should be present. If so, the judgment will show up in some form of manifestation. We should always create with the vision focused forward and seeing the end from the beginning. Yesterday or today and the judgments of yesterday or today do not have to contaminate tomorrow. If we clear judgment from our mind allowing clarity of vision, then we can bring about intentional manifestation .

If you see things and experience things in your life that you do not like or desire, do not judge them. Deal with them, handle them, go through the ups and downs of them, but do not judge it to be the worst, the hardest, or the end. Yes, it is a challenge. It is a change. It is a hard situation, but negates all the facts with your word. For example, stating, "This is not pleasant, it is difficult, but I am doing the best I can and that is enough." "I am pressing through it". "I am growing stronger and learning more". "I am strong". "I am wiser". "I am not what they say or accuse me". "I am only what I say that I am".

Maintain your power to name and redefine. You have the power to speak, create and recreate. Whatever you say, eventually things will have to submit themselves unto the nature you are establishing. Be wise in what you do and what you speak.

God Is No Respecter of Person Or Thought

There was one breath breathed into man. This breath is the central depository energy source. This breath of energy deposited into all things, is the same equal power source. We all have the same potential, the same strength, and the same capacity within us. It is our belief that limits, lives up to, or stretches the limits of our current lives.

Many times, the reason we judge or put people in categories is because we are trying to separate ourselves from the law of limitation we have created or hope is for another and not possible for ourselves. Instead of looking for separation, understand oneness and celebrate others. You should be glad for another and have compassion for them, because what you do for them is done unto you as well. Everything you do is done unto you. Not just the action, but the intent, the energy, and the value. Slavery does not only limit one group, it steals the perfection, evolution, genius and peace that could be experienced by all and limits the growth of even the oppressor. War does not harm just the ones involved, it also has impacts on all governments dealing with upheaval, refugee, and immigration influx, wealth distribution, and protectionist motivations. We are never separated from the hurt, harm or growth of our brothers and sisters in life. We are one and must respect each other as such, because in Spirt there is no separation and no respecter of persons. The respect is only of the Spirit and its integrity and balance of self.

Subconsciously, you already know this. You already know that you are one with all of creation and that no one is any different, because you are begotten of the same source. The only thing that makes you different is what you believe and experience in the vastness of possibilities in the realm of unlimited oneness. You are God and God is you. All that God is you are. All that Christ, the prophets, Muhammad, Buddha, the Sanitarians, Gurus, and the like have done and can do,

Law of First Thought

you can also do, if not greater things. These individuals are not different--they are of one spirit and one mind. Leading the way, loving us, sharing with us, and helping us through their own power of submission and exaltation of a spirit greater than the I. From them and many others, we are learning of their light and possibilities.

Because the examples have already been established and the ways already paved, we only need to heed the word and learn at the feet of those that dared to walk in their greatness despite the voices of dissention that feared them walking in their light. We fear the light of ourselves and others because of the responsibility that comes with it, the ridicule, the yoke, and the potentials that we may not even be able to comprehend. In walking in the fullness of your light and abilities to create, you too will transform your life and the lives of others waiting on you to rise into your greatest possibility. Rise and shine! Your time has come!

Made in the USA
Coppell, TX
29 September 2023